R. M. (Ralph McIntosh) Wilcox

Theory and calculation of cantilever bridges

R. M. (Ralph McIntosh) Wilcox

Theory and calculation of cantilever bridges

ISBN/EAN: 9783337414290

Printed in Europe, USA, Canada, Australia, Japan

Cover: Foto ©Andreas Hilbeck / pixelio.de

More available books at **www.hansebooks.com**

THEORY AND CALCULATION

OF

CANTILEVER BRIDGES.

BY R. M. WILCOX, PH. B.,

Instructor in Civil Engineering in Lehigh University.

NEW YORK
D. VAN NOSTRAND COMPANY
23 MURRAY AND 27 WARREN STREET
1898

PREFACE.

THIS volume replaces the original No. 25 of Van Nostrand's Science Series, bearing the title "Theory and Calculation of Continuous Bridges," by Prof. Mansfield Merriman, which was published in 1875.

The continuous girder, though extensively built in Europe prior to 1875, has now gone entirely out of use, except for revolving draw-bridges, and the cantilever bridge has taken its place. Indeed, the modern cantilever bridge is simply a continuous girder with the chords cut, a form of construction which lacks most of the theoretical objections of its ancestor, and at the same time possesses the very great advantage over simple trusses of erection without false work.

This book has been written with the object of presenting as clearly as possible the theory and methods of calculating the stresses in the trusses of cantilever bridges. Both highway and railroad structures are discussed. In each case a sufficient number of the stresses have been worked out to illustrate the application of the methods, and the stresses in all the members are given in tables.

R. M WILCOX.

South Bethlehem, Pa.,
    March, 1898.

CONTENTS.

CHAPTER I.—*Introduction.*

Art. 1. History of Cantilever Bridges.
" 2. Classification.

CHAPTER II.—*Highway Bridges.*

Art. 3. Definitions.
" 4. Dead Load.
" 5. Reactions Due to Dead Load.
" 6. Shear and Shear Diagrams.
" 7. Moment and Moment Diagrams.
" 8. Cantilevers with Horizontal Chords; Stress in Web Members.
" 9. Cantilevers with Horizontal Chords; Stress in Chord Members.
" 10. Cantilevers with One Chord Inclined.
" 11. Shears and Moments Due to Concentrated Live Load.
" 12. Max. + and − Shear Due to Uniform Live Load.
" 13. Max. + and − Moment Due to Uniform Live Load.
" 14. Cantilever with Horizontal Chords, Uniform Live Load Stresses.

Art. 15. Snow Load and Snow Load Stresses.
" 16. Stresses Due to Wind.
" 17. False Members for Purposes of Erection.
" 18. Final Max. and Min. Stresses.

CHAPTER III.—*Railroad Bridges.*

Art. 19. Loads on Cantilever R. R. Bridges.
" 20. Reaction Due to Dead Load.
" 21. Stresses Due to Dead Load.
" 22. Live Load.
" 23. Live Load Stresses.
" 24. Wind Load Stresses.

CHAPTER I.

INTRODUCTION.

ARTICLE 1.—HISTORY.

THE cantilever bridge is a development of the continuous girder; in fact it is the continuous girder with the chords cut and hinged (properly) at the points of reversion of flexure. The first real practical type of cantilever bridge consisted of two sets of logs projecting out from the two opposite shores of a stream and the space between the ends of these arms spanned by other logs or beams. Such a bridge was built in Thibet about 240 years ago. For a description see R. R. Gazette, 1882, p. 2.

A book entitled "A Treatise on Bridge Architecture," by Thomas Pope, published in New York in 1811, sets forth a scheme for bridging the Hudson river. It was called " Pope's Flying Pendant Lever

Bridge," and contained the principles of the cantilever bridge; but Pope's ideas were decidedly erroneous as regards the stresses.

At a time when tubular bridges and continuous girders were in favor,—about 1850,—it was suggested, by Edwin Clark, that the chords in continuous girders be severed at the points of contrary flexure, and the central portion be hung at those points. This plan though not carried into practical operation until some twenty-five years later, was nevertheless the essential principle of the modern cantilever bridge. In 1833 M. A. Canfield built a bridge at Paterson, N. J., which is claimed to be the first cantilever bridge ever built in America. In 1876–77 C. Shailer Smith built the "Kentucky River Bridge," 300 feet above water. A suspension bridge was originally intended, and towers were built for that purpose. The bridge was built out from the shore panel by panel until the towers were reached, and then continued on until connections were made at the middle. Then, in order to avoid alternate stresses which would be produced if the bridge was perfectly stiff, the chords were cut on the shore arms near the piers. This bridge is located on the Kentucky river, about 112 miles from Cincinnati. For full description see Transactions of the Am. Soc. C. E., Nov. 1878.

In 1867-68 Prof. W. P. Trowbridge, of the School of Mines of Columbia College, New York, conceived of and executed a plan for the first long-span cantilever in America. It was designed to span the East river opposite 76th street, New York, and involved the construction of two immense masonry piers 135 feet high placed on Blackwell's Island. On top of these masonry piers it was intended to place iron towers 150 feet higher. For full description of the proposed bridge see Eng. News, Dec. 29, 1883.

"The Niagara Cantilever Bridge" was begun in April, and completed in December, 1883. It was considered a wonderful piece of engineering, both in the rapidity of construction and obstacles overcome.

It was designed by C. C. Schneider, M. Am. Soc. C. E., and built by the "Central Bridge Works" of Buffalo, N. Y. The principal dimensions are: Length over all 910 feet, each cantilever 375 feet, and central span 120 feet. It has two points of support 25 feet apart at the piers, which are simply iron towers. The structure carried two lines of railroad 299 feet above the surface of the water of Niagara river. A paper on this bridge is to be found in vol. XIV of the Transactions of Am. Soc., C. E.

The next cantilever bridge of importance built in America was the " St. John River Bridge." It was opened for traffic in September, 1885, and was another example of rapid construction. It had the following general dimensions: Total length 812½ feet, two cantilevers of 287 and 382 feet respectively, and a central span of 143½ feet. A full account of this bridge is to be found in R. R. Gazette, 1885, p. 691.

"The Louisville Bridge," over the Ohio river, connecting the cities of Louisville, Ky., and New Albany, Ind., consists of two cantilever spans 480 and 483 feet long respectively, separated by a continuous span of 360 feet; two anchor spans of 260 feet each, a swing span of 370 feet, and a fixed span on the New Albany side of 240 feet—making a total length of 2453 feet. The distance from the under side of the trusses to the water is 95 feet. It was built in 1886, by the Union Bridge Co. under trying difficulties, and was made of open-hearth steel. See Eng. News, Nov. 27, 1886.

"The Poughkeepsie Bridge," over the Hudson river at Poughkeepsie, N. Y., has a total length (not including viaduct approaches) of 3093 feet. It is 212 feet above high water and consists of five spans of continuous and cantilever trusses. It was built by the Union Bridge Co., in 1887-88. The foundations for the piers of this bridge were very deep, one being 129 feet below the surface of the river. See R. R. Gazette, July 1, 1887, and also Eng. News, Oct. 29, 1887.

The " Philadelphia Cantilever Bridge,"

over the Schuylkill river at Market street, completed in 1888, is about 409 feet long and 77 feet wide, and consists of two cantilever spans 166 feet 10¾ inches, and one central span 76 feet long.

The "Great Forth Bridge" was commenced in 1881 and completed in 1890. It crosses the "Firth of Forth" in Scotland, and consists of three gigantic cantilevers connected by two central spans each 350 feet long. The middle cantilever is 1620 feet long, and rests on two supports 260 feet apart. The other two cantilevers are each 1505 feet long, and rest on two supports of 145 feet apart. The total length of the bridge is, therefore, 5330 feet. This length does not include the approaches, which in themselves are immense structures. The maximum distance between piers is 1700 feet, the longest span in the world. The clearance of the central spans above high water is 150 feet. A full history and description of this bridge is given in London Engineering, of 1890, p. 213.

Other important cantilever bridges have been built, principal among which in

America may be mentioned the "Red Rock Cantilever Bridge" in California, and the "Memphis Bridge" at Memphis, Tenn. The former was built in 1890, and its main span is 660 feet long. See R. R. Gazette, April 25, 1890, and Eng. News, Sept. 27 and Oct. 4, 1890. The "Memphis Bridge" was opened for traffic in 1892. Largest span 790 feet. See Eng. News, May 12, 1892.

Article 2.—Classification.

A cantilever bridge, as defined in the Century dictionary, consists of bracket-shaped beam trusses extending inward from their supports and connected at the middle of the span, either directly or by an intermediate span of ordinary construction.

This arrangement is shown in Fig. I, and is the simplest type of the modern cantilever bridge. Various modifications of the arrangement of the trusses exist in cantilever bridges, but all contain the principle of the bracket or arm supporting a weight, which is kept in equilibrium by a counter-weight or reaction.

Cantilever bridges are arbitrarily divided into two general classes, depending upon the arrangement of the supports. The first includes those which have two points of support at the pier, as is shown in Fig. XXIII. The "Niagara Cantilever" and "Great Forth" bridges are examples of this class. The second includes those cantilever bridges which at the pier are supported at a single point. Fig. VII represents the arrangement of the reactions for the second class, and the "St. John River" and "Louisville" bridges are good examples of it. The calculations of the reactions for the two cases is quite different, as will be seen by reference to the formulas in Articles 21 and 5 respectively.

CHAPTER II.

HIGHWAY BRIDGES.

Article 3. — Definitions.

The following definitions of shore arm, river arm, and central span apply generally to both classes of cantilevers, but particularly to the truss arrangement represented by the Niagara cantilever bridge, in which there are two piers and two abutments.

Fig. VII. shows this arrangement of trusses, and reference to it will make the definitions clearer.

Shore arm is that part of the bridge included between the abutment and pier, or AF.

River arm is that part included between the pier and central span, or FJ.

Central span is a simple truss supported by the ends of the river arms. Only one half of the central span is shown in Fig. VII.

All forces acting upward are to be taken as positive, and all forces acting downward negative. Thus a positive reaction is one acting upward, while a negative reaction is downward.

Maximum stress means the greatest possible stress, either positive or negative, that can occur in a member. Minimum stress means the least possible stress of the same nature as the maximum stress, or if possible the greatest stress of the opposite kind. Maximum and minimum represent, therefore, the greatest range of stress.

Shear diagrams are drawn to represent the distribution of shear throughout the bridge due to the position of the load shown, while moment diagrams represent the distribution of moments for the particular position of the load shown.

The plus sign placed before a stress means tension, and the minus sign compression.

Article 4.—Dead Load.

The problem of deducing a general formula for dead load in a cantilever bridge, in order to calculate the dead load stresses, is one very difficult to solve, either theoretically or empirically. There are so many different forms of cantilevers, varying in so many ways, that each one seems to be a distinct problem in itself. With such conditions to contend with, it seems almost impossible to derive a formula for dead load.

No satisfactory formula for dead load in cantilever bridges has ever been found, to the author's knowledge, until very recently. In a little book called "De Pontibus," by J. A. L. Waddell (N. Y., John Wiley & Sons, 1898) is presented a formula or diagram for dead load. From this the dead load for each apex of shore and river arms can be found by means of what is called a "percentage curve." This curve is plotted from values taken from a number of typical cantilever bridges, and represents the ratio of the dead apex load of any panel of the shore and river arms, and the dead apex load of the suspended or central span. It checks with remarkable precision the estimated weight of the proposed North River Bridge at New York. Although Mr. Waddell does not guarantee it to be accurate for all forms of cantilevers, nevertheless, suitable modifications of it can probably be so made, as it seems to be based on the right principle.

In the absence of any formula, the only way to get the dead load is to weigh the material, or get the actual shop weights. This is laborious, and involves the calculation of the stresses in certain members: say the end panel of the river arm, due to half the dead weight of the central span, live load on central span, the effect of wind, together with an assumed weight of the members themselves. If the bridge is a highway bridge, a stress due to snow load should be included. With this maximum stress the members considered are designed (rather roughly at first), and their weight compared with the assumed dead weight. If there is but slight difference between the assumed and actual weights of the members, all well and good; but if too great a difference exists between them, the work should be repeated to the extent necessary for close agreement in assumed and actual weights.

This book is not intended to explain the method of designing bridges, but to show how to calculate the stresses in the members of a cantilever bridge: hence, it is of little importance whether the results obtained are the stresses caused by the actual weight of the bridge and the possible weights which may act upon it. The dead apex loads, therefore, will be assumed, and such values taken as to give simple numerical computation.

Article 5.—Reactions Due to Dead Load.

Let w = load per linear foot.
R_1 = shore reaction.
R_2 = river reaction.
l = length of shore arm.

m = length of river arm.
n = length of central span.
W = total weight on bridge.

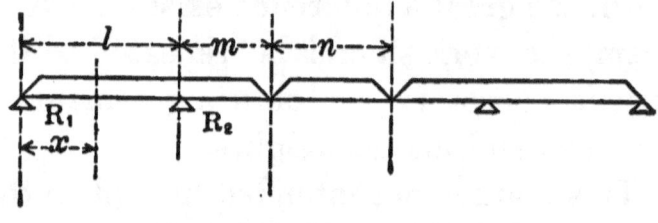

Fig. I

Since one half the weight of the central span, wn, is supported at the end of the river area, the reaction R_2 can be found by taking R_1 as the origin of moments, then

$$R_2 l + \frac{wn}{2}(l+m) + \tfrac{1}{2} w (l+m)^2 = 0,\text{ or}$$

$$R_2 = \frac{wn(l+m) + w(l+m)^2}{2l} \quad \ldots (1)$$

But $R_1 + R_2 = w\left(l+m+\tfrac{n}{2}\right) = W$

and $R_1 = w\left(l+m+\tfrac{n}{2}\right) - R_2 \ldots (2)$

By taking the end of the river arm as the origin of moments, the moment of the forces on the left is

$$R_2 m - \tfrac{1}{2} w (l+m)^2 - R_1(l+m) = 0 \ldots (3)$$

and $R_1 = \dfrac{\frac{1}{2} w (l + m)^2 - R_2 m}{l + m}$ ....(4)

These equations are sufficient to determine the reactions in any cantilever with supports arranged as shown in Fig. I.

R_1 may have a positive, negative, or zero value, depending upon the relative length of l, m and n.

The criterion that R_1 shall equal zero is expressed by the equation $l^2 + m^2 + m n = 0$, from which $l = \sqrt{m^2 + m n}$. When l is greater than $\sqrt{m^2 + m n}$, the value of R_1 is greater than zero, or positive, and acts upward; also, when l is less than $\sqrt{m^2 + m n}$, the value of R_1 is negative, and acts downward.

ARTICLE 6.—SHEAR DUE TO DEAD LOAD.

Since the shear in any section of a beam is equal to the algebraic sum of the vertical forces on the left of that section, it follows that the shear in the shore arm at any section distant x from R_1 (see Fig. I) may be expressed by the equation $R_1 -$

wx. For the river arm the expression for shear in any section distant x from R_1 is, $R_1 + R_2 - wx$. The shear in any section of central span distant x from its left end is $\frac{wn}{2} - wx$.

The distribution of shears due to dead load for the different sections throughout, for the case when l is greater than $\sqrt{m^2 + mn}$ is represented by the diagram of Fig. II., R_1 being positive.

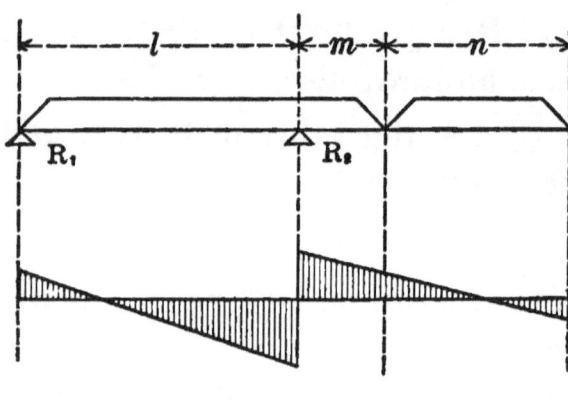

Fig. II

Fig. III shows the distribution of shears for the case when l is less than $\sqrt{m^2 + mn}$, or when R_1 is negative.

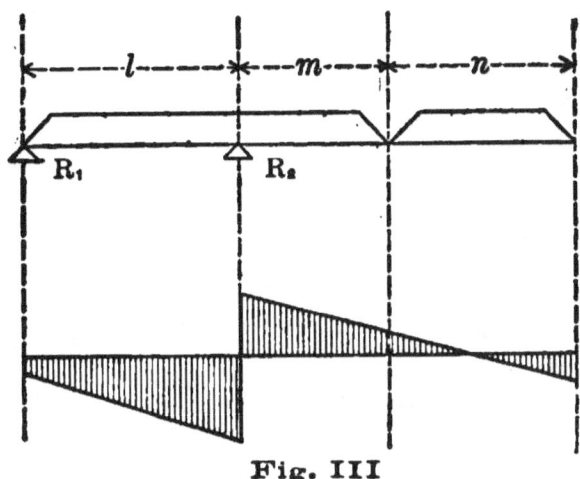

Fig. III

ARTICLE 7.—DEAD LOAD BENDING MOMENT.

In order to find the moment at any section of the shore and river arms, it is necessary first to find the values of R_2 and R_1 from equations (1) and (2). The moment at any section of the shore arm distant x from R_1 is represented by the equation

$$M = R_1 x - \frac{w x^2}{2}.$$

The point of maximum moment is where the vertical shear equals zero. Put the equation for shear $R_1 - w x$ equal to zero, solve for x, and substituting this value of x in the above equation will give the maximum moment in shore arm.

When R_1 is positive there exists, in the shore arm, an inflection point or point at which the moment changes from positive to negative, and is sometimes called the point of reverse flexure. To find where this point is, put $R_1 x - \dfrac{w x^2}{2}$ equal to zero, and solve for x.

The moment in the river arm at any section distant x from R_1 is expressed by

$$M = R_1 x + R_2 (x - l) - \dfrac{w x^2}{2}.$$

This moment is always negative. The same result should be obtained if the moment of the forces on the right of section is taken, or

$$M = \dfrac{w n x}{2} + \dfrac{w x^2}{2},$$ where x is the distance from section to the end of river arm. This is often a simpler equation to use in computation than the former, in which R_1 may be positive or negative according as l is greater

or less than $\sqrt{m^2 + mn}$. This should be determined and the proper sign given to R_1 in the equation of moment of forces on left. In the central span the moment is found just as in the case of a simple beam. The equation of moments at section distant x from its lift end is,

$$M = \frac{wnx}{2} - \frac{wx^2}{2}.$$

The moment diagram for the case when l is greater than $\sqrt{m^2 + mn}$, or when R_1 is positive, is shown in Fig. IV.

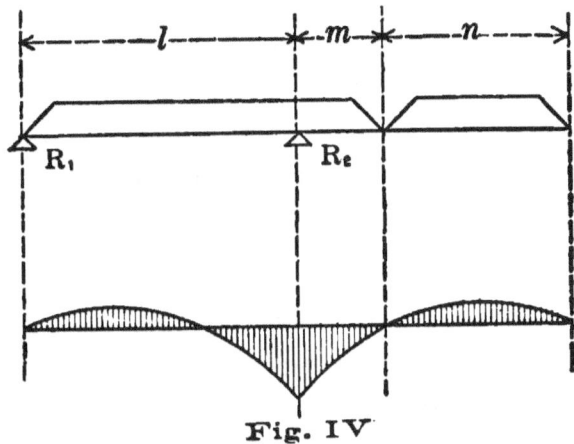

Fig. IV

When R_1 is negative, Fig. V represents the distribution of moments.

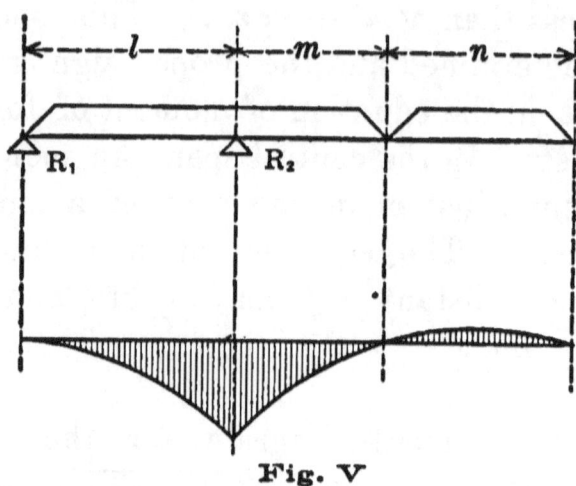

Fig. V

ARTICLE 8.—CANTILEVERS WITH HORIZONTAL CHORDS; STRESSES IN WEB MEMBERS DUE TO DEAD LOAD.

The rule for finding the stress in the web members of a truss with horizontal upper and and lower chords is as follows: *Pass a section cutting the member, the stress in which is to be found, and multiply the shear in the section by the secant of the angle which the member makes with the vertical.*

Let the cantilever shown in Fig. VI have length of shore arm equal to 100 feet, river arm 80 feet, central span 80 feet and depth 16 feet. Then $\sec \theta = 1.18$. Let uniform dead load equal 250 pounds per linear foot, or 5000 pounds per panel.

Fig. VI

$$R_2 = \frac{w\,m\,(l + m) + w\,(l + m)^2}{2\,l}$$

$$R_2 = \frac{250 \times 80 \times 180 + 250 \times 180^2}{200}$$

$$= + 58\,500 \text{ pounds.}$$

$$R_1 = w \left(l + m + \frac{n}{2} \right) - R_2,$$

$R_1 = 250\,(100 + 80 + 40) - 58\,500$
$R_1 = -\,3500$ pounds.

This shows that R_1 is a negative reaction; that is, it acts downward.

The stress in a A equals $(R_1 - P_0)$ sec. θ, or a A $= +\,(3500 + 2500)\,1.18 = +\,7080$ pounds.

A $b = -\,(3500 + 2500)\,1.18 = -\,7080$.
B $c = -\,(3500 + 2500 + 5000)\,1.18$
$= -\,12\,980$ pounds.

$$F g = (- R_1 + R_2 - P_0 - P_1 - \text{etc.}, \ldots\ldots P_8) \sec\theta.$$
$$F g = (- 3500 + 58\,500 - 2500 - 5 \times 5000)\, 1.18 = + 32\,450 \text{ pounds.}$$
$$I j = (- 3500 + 58\,500 - 2500 - 8 \times 5000)\, 1.18 = + 14\,750 \text{ pounds.}$$
$$J j = \frac{w\,n}{2} \sec\theta = 7500 \times 1.18 = - 8850 \text{ pounds.}$$

Enough of the members have been taken to show how the stresses are calculated for web members throughout the bridge due to dead load.

ARTICLE 9.—CANTILEVERS WITH HORIZONTAL CHORDS STRESSES IN CHORD MEMBERS.

There are two methods of finding the stress in the chord members of trusses with horizontal chords : first, by the "Method of Moments"; and, second, by the method of "Chord Increments."

The method of chord increments does not hold good when one of the chords is inclined; so the method of moments will be used in illustrating the calculation of chord stress.

Draw a section cutting three members, take the origin of moments at the intersection of the two members cut, other than the one in which the stress is to be found; then state the equation of moments between the stress and the applied forces on the lift of the section, and solve for the unknown stress.

It is necessary at first to calculate the reactions R_2 and R_1, just as was done in Art. 8. If same example, data, etc., be taken in this case as used in the last article, then $R_2 = 58\,500$ and $R_1 = -3500$ pounds.

Let it be required to find the stress in bc, see Fig. VI. Pass a section cutting A B, B b and bc, and take the origin of moments at B.

The equation of moment is then
$(-R_1 - P_0)\,30 - P_1 \times 10 + bc \times 16 = 0$
$-6000 \times 30 - 5000 \times 10 + bc \times 16 = 0$
and $bc = -14\,375$ pounds.

Take the member D E. The origin of moments is at e and the equation is

$6000 \times 80 - 15\,000 \times 40 + DE \times 16 = 0$
and $DE = +\,51\,875$ pounds.

The origin of moments for the chord member fg is at F, and the equation of moments of the forces on the left and the stress in fg is

$(-R_1 - 2500)\,110 + R_2 \times 10 - 25\,000 \times 50 + fg \times 16 = 0$
$-\,6000 \times 110 + 58\,500 \times 10 - 25\,000 \times 50 + fg \times 16 = 0$

and $fg = -\,82\,813$ pounds.

The moment equation may express the moment of the forces on the right instead of those on the left and it is often a saving of labor to express it in that way; as, for example, to find the stress in H I the origin is at i, and the equation of moments is $HI \times 16 = 12\,500 \times 20$
$HI = 250\,000 \div 16 = +\,15\,625$ pounds.
Stress in $ij = \dfrac{12\,500 \times 10}{16} = +\,7813$ pounds.

The examples given are sufficient to show how the stress in any member of a highway cantilever with horizontal chords, due to dead load, can be found.

ARTICLE 10.—CANTILEVERS WITH ONE CHORD INCLINED. STRESS IN MEMBERS DUE TO DEAD LOAD.

A favorite form of cantilever bridge is that in which one of the chords is inclined. When this arrangement of the chords exists, the principle that the stress in any web member is equal to the shear in the sections, multiplied by the secant of the angle which the member makes with the vertical no longer holds true, for the reason that the inclined chord member takes up a part of the shear.

Let cantilever shown in Fig. VII have length of shore arm equal to 100 feet,

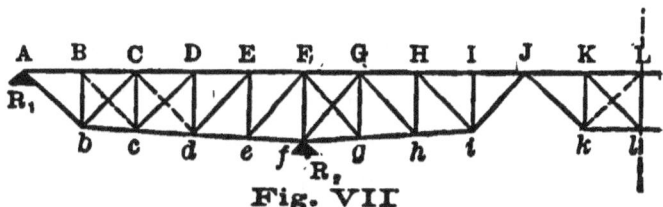

Fig. VII

river arm 80 feet, central span 80 feet, and distance apart of trusses 16 feet; B b = 20 feet, F f = 24 feet, I i = 21 feet and K k = 21 feet. Let the dead load per linear foot be 500 pounds, all on the upper chord.

Since the length of the arms is the same and the load per linear foot double that of the examples given in Art. 8, $R_2 = + 58\,500 \times 2 = +117\,000$ and $R_1 = -3500 \times 2 = -7000$ pounds.

Taking b as the center of moments, the stress in A B is given by the equation $AB \times 20 - R_1 \times 20 - 5000 \times 20 = 0$ and $AB = BC = +12\,000$ pounds.

$Bb = -10\,000$ pounds, or the weight of the apex load that comes upon it.

For the stress in Ab, take the center of moments at B. Then $Ab \times 14.142 = 12\,000 \times 20$ or $Ab = -16\,960$ pounds.

For the stress in the member bC, pass a section through, cutting BC, bC and bc; take the origin of moments at the intersection of BC and bc, which is 420 feet to the left of C and the lever arm of bC is 296.98 feet. The equation of moments of the forces on the left of the section is $bC \times 296.98 = 12\,000 \times 380 + 10\,000 \times 400$ and $bC = +28\,740$ pounds.

The stress in bc is found by taking the

origin of moments at C. The lever arm of bc is 20.97 feet giving the equation $bc \times 20.97 - 12\,000 \times 40 - 10\,000 \times 20 = 0$ and $bc = -32\,400$ pounds.

The origin of moments for Cc is at the intersection of C D and bc, or 420 feet to the left of C, and the equation gives
$-Cc \times 420 + 12\,000 \times 380 + 20\,000 \times 410$
and $Cc = -30\,380$ pounds.

A sufficient number of the members have been taken to illustrate the method of calculating the stress due to uniform load in the members of the shore and river arms.

The member Ff may, however, offer some difficulty if treated according to the method shown. If the section be passed, cutting ef, fg and Ff, the solution becomes very simple by placing the vertical component of the stress in ef, fg and Ff, equal to the reaction R_2. This equation will contain only one unknown quantity Ff, since ef and fg can be computed by the method of moments, and R_2 is known.

The equation is:
$$R_2 = Ff + Vef + Vfg,$$

or $Ff = R_2 - (Vef + Vfg)$,
in which Vef and Vfg represent the vertical components of the stress in ef and fg respectively. These stresses, taken from the table, are 133 600 and 133 500 pounds, and vertical components of them 6680 and 6675 pounds. The above equation for Ff reduces then to
$$Ff = 117\ 000 - (6680 + 6675) =$$
$$-103\ 600 \text{ pounds.}$$
The stress in the members of the central span are calculated just like those of a simple deck truss. Since it has its chords parallel, the stress in any web member is equal to the shear multiplied by the secant of θ.

The stress in all the members of the cantilever truss shown in Fig. VII, due to dead load, are calculated in the manner shown, and the stresses given in the following table. The object in giving the tables of stresses complete, throughout the book, is to have them serve as answers to any self-selected problem that the student may take. For instance, if the student wishes to test his ability in working out the stress in any member not already given he may take for example F G and apply the same principles as used in finding the stress in A B, and verify his result from the table.

If the student will pursue this course it will be found to be of very great help to him in better understanding the problems.

Dead Load Stresses for Cantilever shown in Fig. VII.

Member.	Stress in Pounds.	Member.	Stress in Pounds.
AB = BC	+ 12000	kl	+ 14280
CD	+ 32380	Bb	− 10000
DE	+ 60000	bC	+ 28820
EF	+ 94000	Cc	− 30400
FG	+ 91300	cD	+ 40120
GH	+ 54550	Dd	− 39000
HI = IJ	+ 23800	dE	+ 50450
JK	− 14280	Ee	− 47300
KL	− 19050	eF	+ 6000
Ab	− 16960	Ff	−103650
bc	− 32460	Fg	+ 64090
cd	− 60000	gG	− 50440
de	− 94040	Gh	+ 54700
ef	−133600	hH	− 42280
fg	−133500	Hi	+ 44650
gh	− 91400	iI	− 1000
hi	− 54600	kK	− 15000
iJ	− 34530	Kl	+ 6900
Jk	+ 20700	Ll	− 10000

ARTICLE 11. — SHEARS AND MOMENTS DUE TO CONCENTRATED LIVE LOAD.

In addition to the dead and snow load, cantilever bridges are subjected to a live load stress. This live load consists, in the case of highway bridges, of foot people, horses and wagons, electric cars, etc.

In order to determine the maximum and minimum stress in all the members affected by this load, involves a knowledge of the proper position of live load to produce it. What, then, is the possible arrangement of the live load? Unlike the dead load, the live load may occupy a part of, or different parts of, the bridge at the same time; it may also, like the dead load, cover the entire bridge at once.

It is necessary, therefore, to consider all possible arrangements of the live load, and to find that position for it which will produce the maximum and minimum shear and moment for any section.

Consider first, one concentrated load, P, which is in the nature of an electric car or heavily loaded wagon.

(a) For a load P on the shore arm,

$$R_1 = \frac{Pl'}{l}, \text{ and } R_2 = \frac{P(l-l')}{l} \quad \ldots \ldots (5)$$

The effect is just like a load P on a simple beam, and the distribution of shears and moments is as shown in Fig. VIII.

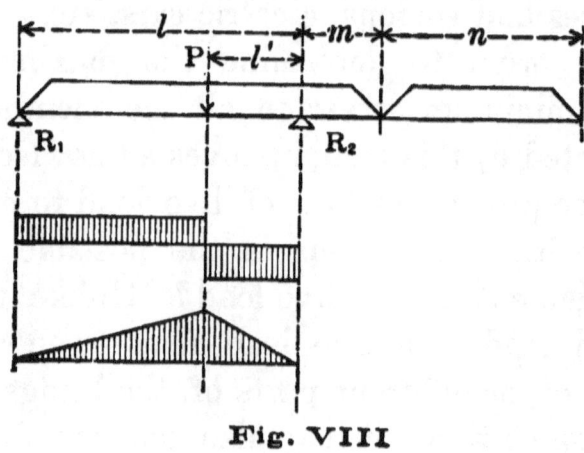

Fig. VIII

(b) For a load P on river arm,

$$R_1 = -\frac{Pm'}{l}, \text{ and } R_2 = \frac{P(l+m')}{l} \quad \ldots \ldots (6)$$

and the shears and the moments are distributed as shown in Fig. IX.

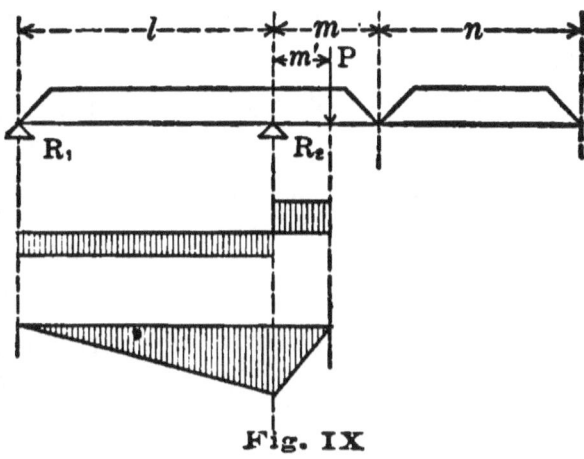

Fig. IX

(c) For load P on central span,

$$R_1 = -P\frac{n'}{n} \cdot \frac{m}{l}, \text{ and } R_2 = P\frac{n'}{n}\left(\frac{l+m}{l}\right) .. (7)$$

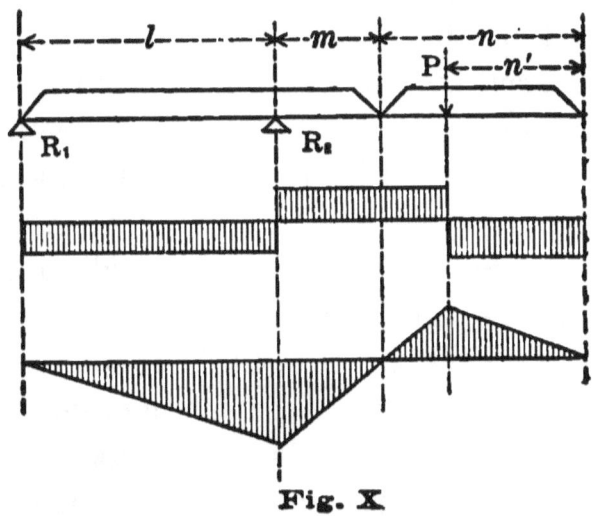

Fig. X

and Fig. x. shows distribution of shears and moments.

An examination of the shear diagrams in the three cases (*a*), (*b*) and (*c*) shows that the maximum positive shear in any section, due to a load P, occurs when the load is placed just to the right of the section, and that the maximum negative shear occurs when the load is placed just to the left of the section.

An examination of the moment diagrams shows that, for case (*a*), the moment is positive, and is a maximum for any section in *l*, when P is over the section; that, for case (*b*), a negative moment is produced in the shore arm and negative in river arm, both increasing as m' increases, and having a maximum value when $m' = m$, or when P is placed at the end of the river arm; and that, in case (*c*), a negative moment is produced in both the shore and river arms, and a positive moment in the central span; also that the shore and river arm moments are a maximum when P is placed at the left end of the central span, and a maximum in any section of the central span when P is over the section.

The above conclusions are given, in condensed form, in the following table:

Table showing Position of Load P to give Maximum Positive and Negative Moments.

	Case (a). P on Shore Arm.	Case (b). P on River Arm.	Case (c). P on Central Span.
Moment in l.	$+\begin{cases} \text{Max.} \\ \text{when P is} \\ \text{over the} \\ \text{Section.} \end{cases}$	$-\begin{cases} \text{Max.} \\ \text{when P is} \\ \text{at } m'=m \end{cases}$	$-\begin{cases} \text{Max.} \\ \text{when P is} \\ \text{at } n'=n. \end{cases}$
Moment in m.	0	$-\begin{cases} \text{Max.} \\ \text{when P is} \\ \text{at } m'=m \end{cases}$	$-\begin{cases} \text{Max.} \\ \text{when P is} \\ \text{at } n'=n. \end{cases}$
Moment in n.	0	0	$+\begin{cases} \text{Max.} \\ \text{when P is} \\ \text{over} \\ \text{Section.} \end{cases}$

Table showing Position of Load P for Maximum Positive and Negative Shears.

	Max. + Shear.	Max. − Shear.
Shore Arm.	P just to right of Section.	P just to left of Section.
River Arm.	P at end of River Arm.	None.
Central Span.	P just to right of Section.	P just to left of Section.

Article 12.—Maximum + and — Shear Due to Uniform Live Load.

The diagrams of shears and moments in the preceding article represent the effect of a single load P.

The effect of any number of loads, as P_1, P_2, P_3, etc., may be shown in the same manner, the resulting diagram being the same as the combined diagrams for each load taken separately.

When these loads act sufficiently close together and are of the same intensity, the result is a uniformly distributed load. Such a load is represented in highway bridges by a mass of foot-people moving in a continuous or broken line across the bridge. It is necessary, therefore, to consider the effect of such load, and the position or possible arrangement of it to give the maximum + and — shear and moment at any section.

The live load in highway bridges may consist of both concentrated and uniform load, acting at the same time on different parts of the bridge. This combination is not, however, generally made in highway bridges, as the result is not as injurious as that due to the full uniform load. If such a combination should be desired, the rules of Art. 11, 12 and 13 are to be followed.

The shearing effect of uniform live load will now be considered.

For any section in the shore arm, the greatest positive shear occurs when the load is so placed as to give to R_1 the greatest possible positive value, with no load on the left of the section to subtract from it.

Any load on the river arm and central span causes a negative reaction at R_1; therefore, the maximum positive shear in any section of the shore arm occurs when the shore arm is covered with the uniform load to the right of the section, which makes

$$V = R_1 = \frac{w\, l'^2}{2l} \quad \dots\dots\dots\dots\dots\dots(8)$$

and gives a shear diagram, as shown in Fig. XI.

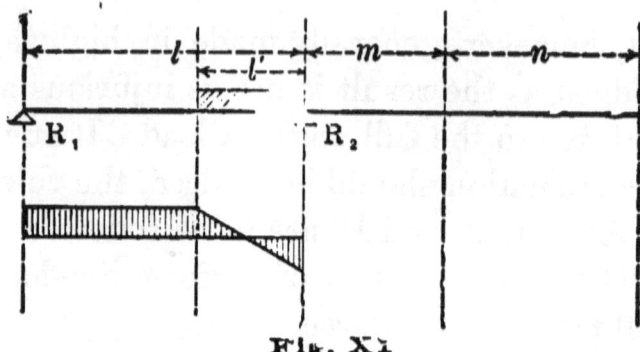

Fig. XI

In the river arm, the maximum positive shear for any section occurs when the load covers the central span and the river arm to right of the section.

$$\text{Then } R_1 = \frac{wmn}{2l} + \frac{wm'\left(m - \frac{m'}{2}\right)}{l},$$

$$\text{and } R_2 = \frac{wn(m+l)}{2l} + \frac{wm'\left(l + m - \frac{m'}{2}\right)}{l}$$

Since $V = -R_1 + R_2$, substituting for R_1 and R_2 their values as given above, and reducing, gives

$$V = \frac{wn}{2} + wm' \quad \dots \dots \dots (9)$$

which equation is also the algebraic sum of the vertical forces on the right of the section.

The position of load for maximum positive shear, for any section of river arm, is shown in Fig. XII.

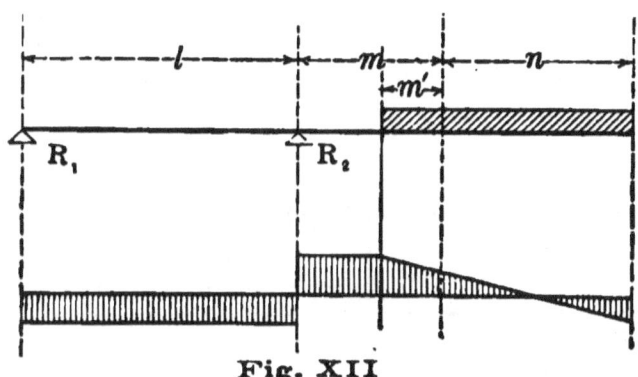

Fig. XII

In order to obtain the greatest negative shear in any section of the shore arm, it is apparent, from the equation $V = R_1 - wx$, that R_1 should have the greatest negative value possible. Since R_1 is negative due to the live load on the river arm and central span, it is evident that the proper position of live load to fulfill the condition is, to cover the river arm and central span with the uniform load, and also the shore arm to the left of the section.

The value of R_1 is found from the equation

$$R_1 = + \frac{wx\left(l - \frac{x}{2}\right)}{l} - \frac{wm^2}{2l} - \frac{wmn}{2l}$$

and the shear from
$$V = R_1 - wx \dots \dots \dots \dots (10)$$

The position of load and shear diagram is shown in Fig. XIII.

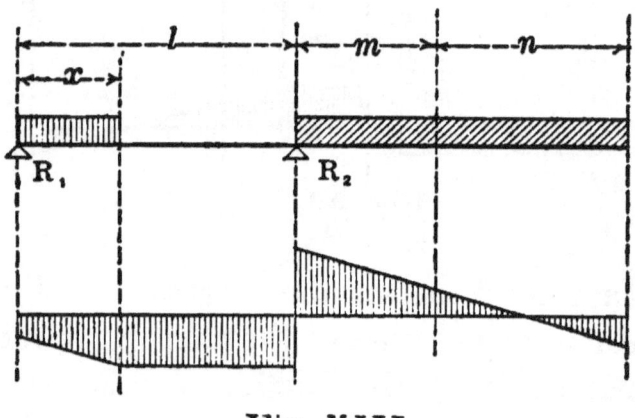

Fig. XIII

In the river arm there is no negative shear due to live load. In other words, there is no possible arrangement of the load to produce a negative shear in the river arm. A load on left of section gives
$$V = R_1 + R_2 - wm = 0.$$

The maximum positive shear in central span for any section, occurs when load is on the right of the section; maximum negative, when central span is loaded on the left of section, just as in the case of a simple beam.

Table giving Positions of Uniform Live Load to Give Max. Positive and Negative Shears.

	Max. + Shear.	Max. − Shear.
Shore Arm.	Load to cover Shore Arm right of Section.	Load on River Arm and Central Span, also Shore Arm, left of Section.
River Arm.	Load on Central Span and River Arm, right of Section.	None.
Central Span.	Right of Section.	Left of Section.

ARTICLE 13.—MAXIMUM POSITIVE AND NEGATIVE MOMENT DUE TO UNIFORM LIVE LOAD.

The position of live load to produce maximum moment in any section of the shore arm is when the live load covers the entire shore arm.

The equation of bending moment at

any section distant x from the left end is $R_1 x - \dfrac{wx^2}{2}$.

Substituting for R_1 its value $\dfrac{wl}{2}$ in the above equation gives

$$M = \frac{wlx}{2} - \frac{wx^2}{2} \quad \dots\dots\dots\dots(11)$$

If any live load is placed on the river arm or central span, its effect is to produce a negative value in R_1, thereby decreasing the value of M.

The diagram in Fig. XIV shows the distribution of maximum positive moments for the shore arm.

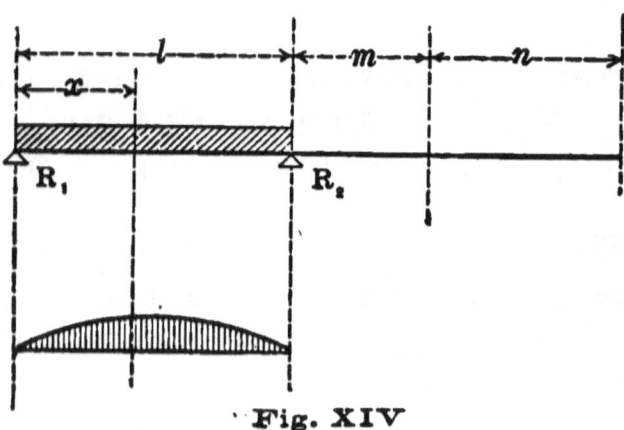

Fig. XIV

There is no position of the live load that will give a positive moment in the river arm; the moment in the river arm is always negative.

The central span being like a simple beam, its maximum positive moment for any section occurs when it is fully loaded, as shown in Fig. XV, in which

$$M = \frac{wnx}{2} - \frac{wx^2}{2} \quad \ldots\ldots\ldots\ldots(12)$$

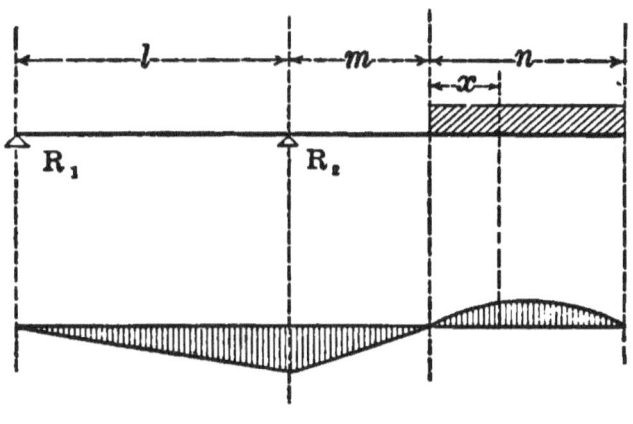

Fig. XV

The maximum negative moment in the shore arm will evidently occur when the load is so placed as to give the greatest negative value for R_1, and to have no load on the shore arm to cause a positive value for R_1. To produce this result, the river arm and central span should be fully loaded and no load on the shore arm.

The diagram of moments is shown in Fig. XVI, and the value of the moment is found from

$$M = - R_1 x \quad \ldots\ldots\ldots\ldots\ldots(13)$$

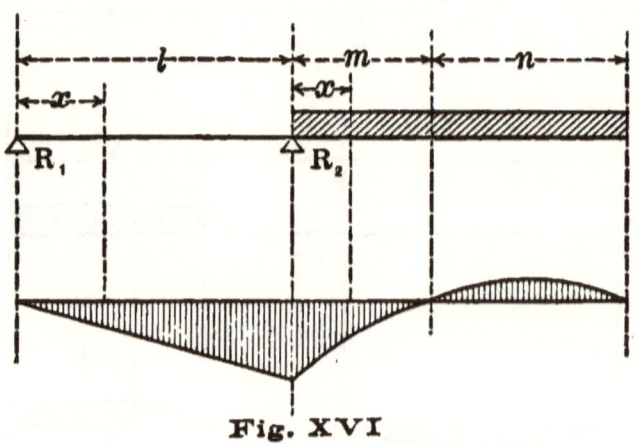

Fig. XVI

The position of load to produce maximum negative moments in river arm is of course that which will produce the greatest negative value of R_1. This will occur when the river arm and central span are loaded, with no load on shore arm, as in Fig. XVI. The equation of moments for any section in river arm distant x from R_2 is $M = - R_1 (l + x) - \dfrac{w x^2}{2} + R_2 x.$

The moment at the section due to that part of the load on the left of the section is zero; consequently, the quantity $-\dfrac{wx^2}{2}$ in the above equation becomes zero if the load is placed on the central span and on the right of the section only in the river arm. The effect is the same, and the above equation is simplified to

$$M = - R_1 (l + x) + R_2 x \ldots\ldots(14)$$

and the diagram of moments for this position is shown in Fig. XVII.

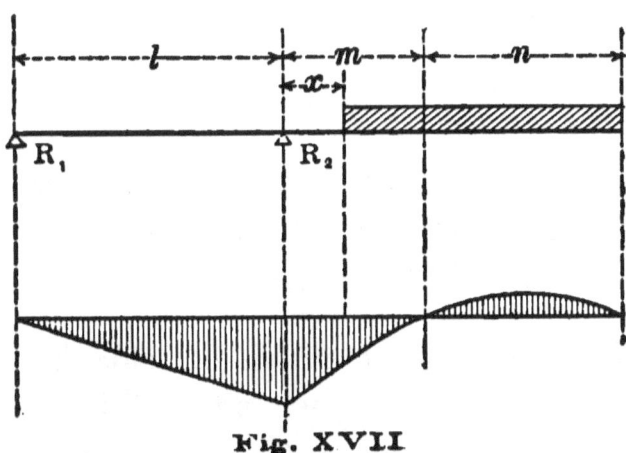

Fig. XVII

There is no negative moment possible in the central span, since it is a simple truss.

The following table gives, in condensed form, the position of live load for max. positive and negative moments in the different parts of cantilevers.

Table Showing Position of Uniform Live Load to Give Maximum + and − Moments.

	Max. + Moment.	Max. − moment.
Shore Arm (*l*).	Load on entire Shore Arm.	Load on entire River Arm and Central Span.
River Arm (*m*).	No + moment possible.	Load on Central Span and River Arm, right of Section.
Central Span (*n*)	Load on entire Central Span.	No − moment possible.

ARTICLE 14.—CANTILEVER BRIDGE WITH HORIZONTAL CHORD; STRESSES DUE TO UNIFORM LIVE LOAD.

To illustrate method of calculating stresses in a cantilever due to live load, let same example as given in Article 3 be taken. Shore arm 100 feet, river arm 80 feet, central span 80 feet, and depth of truss 16 feet. Secθ = 1.18. Let live load be taken at 70 pounds per square foot of floor surface. Assuming the bridge to be 30 feet wide, the weight per linear foot for one truss is 70 × 15 = 1050 pounds. This multiplied by the panel length 20 feet gives 21 000, or say 20 000 pounds, as the live panel load which is all applied to the chord that supports the floor system.

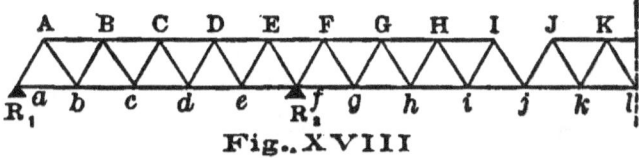

Fig. XVIII

To find the stress in Aa caused by the maximum positive and maximum negative shear. For maximum positive shear, load covers shore arm on right of section, (see table in Art. 12). R_1 = 2 × 20 000 = 40 000 pounds.

Stress in Aa = 40 000 × 1.18 = — 47 200 pounds. For maximum negative shear, oad covers river arm, central span, and shore arm left of section.

$$R_1 = \frac{60\,000 \times 40 + 50\,000 \times 80}{100}.$$

$$R_1 = -64\,000 \text{ pounds.}$$

Shear $= V = -R_1 = -64\,000$ pounds.

Stress in $Aa = 64\,000 \times 1.18 = +75\,520$ pounds.

For stress in Gh due to maximum positive shear, the live load covers central span and river arm on the right of section. The panel points loaded are h, i, j, k and l.

$$\text{Then} -R_1 = \frac{40\,000 \times 50 + 50\,000 \times 80}{100}$$

$$R_1 = -60\,000.$$

From (2) $R_1 + R_2 = W$, therefore $-60\,000 + R_2 = 90\,000$ and $R_2 = +150\,000$ pounds.

V in $Gh = -60\,000 + 150\,000 = 90\,000$ and stress in $Gh = 90\,000 \times 1.18 = +106\,200$ pounds.

There is no negative shear possible in river arm; therefore, no compressive stress in Gh.

For the stresses in CD the maximum positive moment will be first considered,

and this occurs by reference to table in Art. 13, when live load covers the entire shore arm. $R_1 = 2 \times 20\,000 = 40\,000$ pounds, and center of moments is at d, then
$$CD = \frac{40\,000 \times 60 - 40\,000 \times 30}{16}$$
$$= -75\,000 \text{ pounds.}$$

Maximum negative moment for section through C D occurs when river arm and central span is loaded.

For this position of load,
$$R_1 = \frac{60\,000 \times 40 + 50\,000 \times 80}{100}$$
and $R_1 = -64\,000$
$$CD = \frac{64\,000 \times 60}{16} = +240\,000 \text{ pounds.}$$

Take the lower chord member of the river arm, ij. There is no positive moment possible, so the maximum negative moment alone will be considered. This takes place when live load covers central span and river arm on right of section.
$$R_1 = -\frac{50\,000 \times 80}{100} = -40\,000 \text{ pounds.}$$
$R_2 = +90\,000$ pounds.

With center of moments at J, stress in ij equals

$$\frac{-40\,000 \times (100 + 70) + 90\,000 \times 70}{16}$$

$$ij = -31\,250 \text{ pounds.}$$

The following is perhaps a shorter and more rapid method of calculating the reactions in a cantilever truss, due to live load, than the one just used.

Let P_0, P_1, P_2, P_3, etc., be the panel loads at the apex points, a, b, c, d, etc., of the truss shown in Fig. XVIII. Then, since $5/5$ of P_0 is supported by R_1, $4/5$ of P_1 goes to R_1 and $3/5$ of P_2 etc., goes to the same reaction, a table of coefficients can be formed giving the part of each load supported by R_1 and R_2.

If, then, the load is placed in the proper position for maximum, positive, and negative shear or moments, the reaction R_1, due to the loads on the required panel points is found by adding together the product obtained by multiplying each panel load by its coefficient in the column R_1. In the same way the value of R_2 can be found. This applies to loads on the river arm and central span, as well as to loads on the shore arm.

Load.	Part Supported by R_1.	Part Supported by R_2.
P_0	$+1. \times P_0$	$0. \times P_0$
P_1	$+0.8 \times P_1$	$+0.2 \times P_1$
P_2	$+0.6$ etc.	$+0.4$ etc.
P_3	$+0.4$	$+0.6$
P_4	$+0.2$	$+0.8$
P_5	$0.$	$+1.$
P_6	-0.2	$+1.2$
P_7	-0.4	$+1.4$
P_8	-0.6	$+1.6$
P_9	-0.8	$+1.8$
P_{10}	-0.8	$+1.8$
P_{11}	-0.8	$+1.8$

To find the stress in Gh, the load covers the river arm and central span to the right of section or apex points h, i, j, k and l, are loaded each with 20 000 pounds, except that at l, which is one half or $\frac{20\,000}{2}$. Then by the use of the table R, is found to be

$20\,000\,(-.4 - .6 - 8, - 8,) + 10\,000 \times - .8 = - 60\,000.$ and R_2 is $20\,000\,(+ 1.4 + 1.6 + 1.8 + 1.8) + 10\,000 \times + 1.8 = + 150\,000$ then $V = - 60\,000 + 150000 = + 90000$ and stress in $Gh = 90\,000 \times 1.18 = 106\,200$ pounds, the same value as that found by the other method.

This method has its greatest advantage when the loads are unequal, or when a uniform live load with excess loads is used, as will be shown in the discussion of live load in railroad bridges.

ARTICLE 15. — SNOW LOAD AND SNOW LOAD STRESSES.

In addition to dead and live loads, highway bridges are subjected to another kind of vertical load, at times in certain climates; namely, snow load. This varies according to climate from 0 to 20 pounds per square foot of floor surface (see Roofs & Bridges, Merriman's and Jacoby, Part I, Art. 41.) Snow load is assumed to be distributed uniformly over the floor surface, and consequently acts on the members of the truss in the same manner as the dead load.

This fact makes the calculation of snow load stresses an easy matter, if the dead load stresses are known.

Let w be the dead load and w' the snow load per linear foot per truss; S the stress in a member due to dead load, and S' the stress in the same member due to snow load, then

$$\frac{w}{w'} = \frac{S}{S'}, \text{ and } S' = S\frac{w'}{w} \quad \ldots\ldots\ldots\ldots\ldots(15)$$

To find the stresses due to snow load, multiply the dead load stresses by the ratio between dead and snow load. It is to be borne in mind that the dead load always acts, while the snow load may or may not act; and although the stresses are of the same nature, they are kept separate in order that the maximum and minimum stresses due to dead, live, snow and wind loads combined may be determined, as is shown in the table of maximum and minimum stresses at the end of the chapter.

Assuming the snow load to be 15

pounds per square foot of floor surface, the snow load per linear foot per truss for the cantilever of Article 10 is if the distance of trusses apart be 16 feet and there are two sidewalks each 5 feet wide outside of the trusses, $\frac{15(16+5+5)}{2} = \frac{390}{2}$ or say 200 pounds per linear foot per truss.

The stress in A b due to snow load is S' = $S \frac{w'}{w}$ = $16960 \frac{200}{500}$ = 6780 pounds.

ARTICLE 16.—STRESSES DUE TO WIND.

To counteract the effect of wind, which, acting horizontally, tends to deflect the truss in a horizontal plane, just as the vertical forces tend to deflect the truss in a vertical plane, members called struts are introduced, extending from the chord apex point of one truss to the same apex point of the other truss, and also tension members or tie-rods extending from the chord apex point of one truss to the next apex point of the other truss. The arrangement of the members of this lateral system is like the members of a Pratt truss, as shown in Fig. XIX.

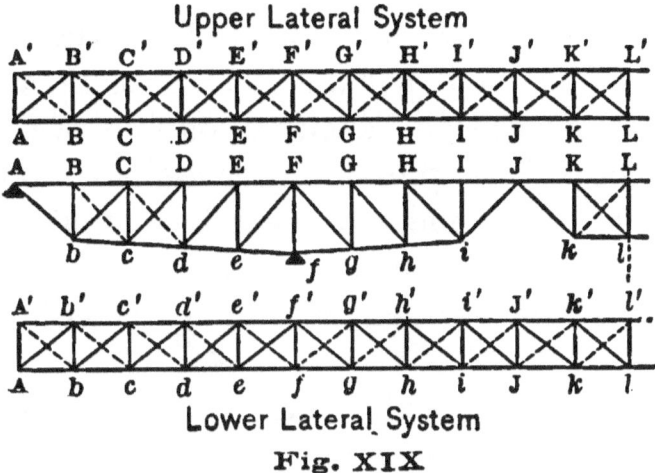

Fig. XIX

The wind blowing in one direction stresses one system, and blowing in the opposite direction stresses the other. This arrangement causes the diagonal member to take tension only.

The actual surface exposed to wind in the cantilever bridge is an unknown quantity before the bridge is designed; therefore, some approximate value must be assumed in order that the stresses due to wind may be calculated. A closely approximate wind load is found for simple trusses (see Merriman's Roofs and Bridges Part I, Art. 42,) by assuming the members of the truss to be each one foot wide; then the total area exposed to wind is twice as many square feet as there are linear feet in the skeleton outline of the truss. The pressure per square foot exerted by wind may be taken at about 30 pounds, although a pressure as high as 40 pounds per square foot is sometimes taken.

Wind load on the truss is taken as acting uniformly over the entire length. It is therefore similar to the dead load, except that it acts horizontally and produces tension in the leeward chords and compression in the windward chords. The stresses in the horizontal system effected by wind are calculated just as the stresses would be for a Pratt truss system. The distribution of shears and moments due to wind on truss is represented by the diagrams of shears and moments due to dead load, shown in Figs. II, III, IV and V.

The wind on the upper chord apex points is transmitted by the upper lateral system of truss shown in Fig. XIX, directly to the abutments and piers. That on the lower chord is transmitted to the piers at one end, and to the abutment at the other, by means of the inclined end posts.

The wind-load stresses given in the table have been calculated as follows: (The results are necessarily an approximation, since the true area exposed to wind is not known.) The skeleton outline of the cantilever, Fig. XIX (dimensions of which are given in Art. 10), is about 1070 feet. Assuming the wind pressure per square foot at 30 pounds, the total wind pressure on one truss is

$$1070 \times 30 = 32\,120 \text{ pounds.}$$

Assuming two-thirds to be applied to the upper chord, since it carries the floor system, and one-third to the lower chord, gives

$$\frac{2 \times 32\,120}{3 \times 11} = 1946,$$

$$\text{and } \frac{1 \times 32\,120}{3 \times 11} = 973 \text{ pounds}$$

respectively for the upper and lower chord apex wind loads. To be on the side of safety, and giving at the same time better values for computation, these may be increased to 2000 and 1000 pounds respectively.

To find the stresses in the upper lateral system (see Fig. XIX), proceed as follows:

$$R_2 \times 100 = 8 \times 4000 \times \frac{180}{2} + 10\,000 \times 180.$$

$R_2 = 28\,800 + 18\,000 = 46\,800$ pounds, and $R_1 \times 100 = 4 \times 4000 \times 50 - 10\,000 \times 80$
$\qquad - 3 \times 4000 \times 40.$

$R_1 = -4800.$

Let $\theta' =$ angle which diagonals in upper lateral system make with the vertical; then secant θ', $= 1.6$ and tan $\theta' = 1.25$.

Stress in A′ B equals $4800 \times 1.6 = +7680$ pounds.

Stress in C D

$$= \frac{4800 \times 40 + 4000 \times 20}{16} = 17\,000$$

for wind West, and 33 000 for wind East.

For C′ D the wind blows West and the shear is $-4800 - 4000 - 4000 = 12\,800$

pounds. This multiplied by the secant of the angle C' D D' gives + 12 800 × 1.6 = + C' D = + 20 480 pounds.

When the wind blows in the opposite direction, or East, the member C D' is stressed an equal amount + 20 480 pounds.

The effect of the wind on the upper chord is to turn the bridge over, as in

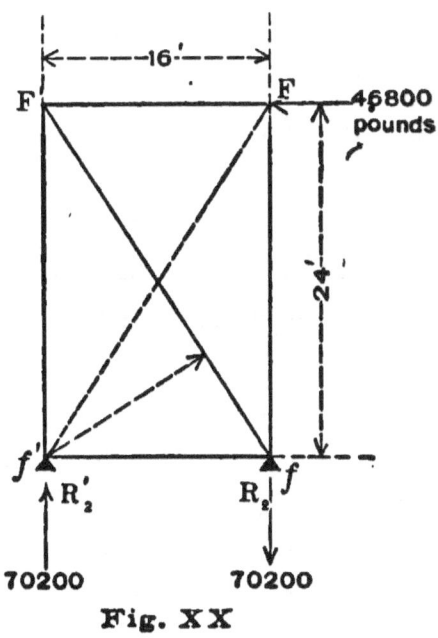

Fig. XX

Fig. XX, which is a cross-section of truss shown in Fig. XIX at Ff. The total wind force acting at F is 46 800 pounds, and, if the two trusses are rigidly connected by members Ff' and $F'f$ and struts, this force of 46 800 pounds tends to produce rotation about the point f', and is held in equilibrium by a downward force R_2 of 70 200 pounds. The equation of moments about f' is

$$-46\,800 \times 24 + 70\,200 \times 16 = 0.$$

The same result obtains if the center of moments be considered as midway between R_2 and R'_2, which latter act as a couple.

If the dead-load reaction R_2 is less than the value R_2, the downward force necessary to produce equilibrium, the bridge will overturn. R_2 due to dead load is 117 000; therefore there is a good factor of safety against overturning, due to the assumed wind pressure of 30.84 pounds per square foot, since in order to overturn the bridge the wind would have to exert a pressure per square foot equal to

$$\frac{117\,000 \times 16 \times 30.84}{46\,800 \times 24} = 51.4 \text{ lbs.}$$

The members $F'f$ and Ff', known as cross-bracing, are designed to take tension only. The stress in $F'f$ is found as follows: Take the center of moments at f', and state the equation of moments.

$$-46\,800 \times 24 + F'f \times p = 0$$
$$p = 16 \times \cos fFf' = 16 \times .83 = 13.28.$$

Therefore, $F'f = \dfrac{46\,800 \times 24}{13.28} = +84\,580 \text{ lbs.}$

In the table of final maximum and minimum stresses, the stresses due to overturning effect of wind on truss are not given, and are omitted, because their effect is so small as not to materially change the final results. The stresses due to overturning effect of wind on truss and train are given in the table of final maximum and minimum stresses in a railroad cantilever bridge and the method of calculation given in Art. 25.

In actual practice it would be well to compare the assumed apex wind loads with the actual wind apex loads as the result of multiplying the assumed pressure in pounds per square foot by the actual surface exposed in the designed structure.

This should be done at least to make sure that the assumed wind apex loads are on the side of safety.

Stresses in Lateral Systems due to Wind.

Member.	Wind East.	Wind West.	Member.	Wind East.	Wind West.
A A'	− 3800	− 3800	H' I	+ 22 400	0
B B'	− 6800	− 6800	I' J	+ 16 000	0
C C'	− 10 800	− 10 800	J' K	+ 9200	0
D D'	− 14 800	− 14 800	K' L	+ 3200	0
E E'	− 18 800	− 18 800	A' b	0	+ 4870
F F'	− 44 800	− 44 800	A b'	+ 4870	0
G G'	− 20 000	− 20 000	b' c	0	+ 6640
H H'	− 16 000	− 16 000	b c'	+ 6640	0
I I'	− 12 000	− 12 000	c' d	0	+ 10 240
J J'	− 5000	− 5000	c d'	+ 10 240	0
K K'	− 4000	− 4000	d' e	0	+ 13 440
L L'	0	− 2000	d e'	+ 13 440	0
A' B	0	+ 7680	e' f	0	+ 16 640
B' C	0	+ 14 080	e f'	+ 16 640	0
C' D	0	+ 20 480	i' J'	0	+ 8 000
D' E	0	+ 26 880	i' J	+ 8 000	0
E' F	0	+ 33 280	h i'	0	+ 11 200
F G'	0	+ 35 200	h' i	+ 11 200	0
G H'	0	+ 28 800	g h'	0	+ 14 200
H I'	0	+ 22 400	g' h	+ 14 200	0
I J'	0	+ 16 000	f g'	0	+ 17 600
J K'	0	+ 9200	f' g	+ 17 600	0
K L'	0	+ 3200	b b'	− 3400	− 3400
A B'	+ 7680	0	c c'	− 5400	− 5400
B C'	+ 14 080	0	d d'	− 7400	− 7400
C D'	+ 20 480	0	e e'	− 9400	− 9400
D E'	+ 26 880	0	f f'	− 22 400	− 22 400
E F'	+ 33 280	0	g g'	− 10 000	− 10 000
F' G	+ 35 200	0	h h'	− 8 000	− 8 000
G' H	+ 28 800	0	i i'	− 6 000	− 6000

Article 17. — False Members Introduced for Purposes of Erection.

The principal advantage that the cantilever bridge possesses over other forms of bridges, the suspension bridge excepted, consists in its economy of erection under unfavorable conditions. Comparatively little false work is required. The bridge is erected by beginning at the pier, and building out on both the shore and river arms until the abutment is reached on one side, and connection made at the middle of the central span on the other.

In order to make connection in the middle it is necessary that the central span or a part of it be made, temporarily, a continuation of the river arm; by means of false members introduced merely to support the arm and the necessary apparatus, etc., used in erection.

It is readily seen that, in the case of the cantilever shown in Fig. VII, the compression member extending from i to j and j to k with a vertical member $J\ j$, would make the central span, or as much of it as is necessary, a part of the river arm of the cantilever.

This change in the arrangement of the members causes a change in the nature and magnitude of stress in some of the members of the truss.

What this change is remains to be determined; so that, if necessary, provision may be made in the cross-section of the members effected to safely erect the bridge.

Fig. XXI represents the skeleton diagram of Fig. VII changed by the false members ij, jk and Jj being introduced for purposes of erection.

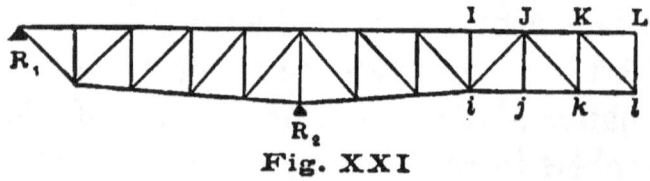

Fig. XXI

The dimensions of truss are the same as that of Fig. VII, and dead apex loads the same, 10 000 pounds; but the live load will be assumed to consist of a single concentrated weight to represent a traveler used in erection. This will be taken at 40 000 pounds. Secant of angle which K l and J k, etc. make with vertical is 1.38.

The position farthest out on the arm that the traveler is likely to occupy is at K, since all the members L l, K l, $k\,l$ etc., are erected with it in that position and connection made. This position gives greatest moment, and consequently greatest stress in all chord members, to the left.

The stress in Ll is — 10 000, pounds due to dead load. K l = 10 000 × 1.38 = + 13 800 pounds. $k\,l = \dfrac{10\,000 \times 20}{21} = -$ 9520 pounds. K k = — 10 000 — 10 000 — 40 000 = — 60 000 pounds, which is greater than the maximum stress due to dead snow and live load as given in table. J k = — 60 000 × 1.38 = + 82 800 pounds. $j\,k = i\,j = + \dfrac{50\,000 \times 20 + 10\,000 \times 40}{21} =$ — 66 660 pounds. i J = 70 000 × 1.38 = — 96 600 pounds. When the traveler is brought over the point I the stress in I i is — 40 000 + 10 000 = — 50 000 pounds.

No change takes place in any other

members throughout the truss, at least to the extent of changing the maximum and minimum stresses due to dead snow and live load. The following table shows what members are stressed during erection greater than when subjected to dead snow and live load.

In addition to the stress due to wind on the truss there may be stress, due to wind on the traveler, which amounts to considerable, depending of course upon its position and the amount of surface exposed.

Possible Stresses During Erection.

Member	Dead Load.	Traveler.	Wind.	Maximum
L l	− 10 000	0	0	− 10 000
K l	+ 13 800	0	0	+ 13 800
K k	− 20 000	− 40 000	0	− 60 000
J k	+ 27 600	+ 55 200	0	+ 82 800
J j	{Assumed. + 2000	0	0	+ 2000
J i	− 41 400	− 55 200	0	− 96 600
I i	− 10 000	− 40 000	0	− 50 000
K L	0	0	± 6400	± 6400
J K	+ 9520	0	± 12 800	+ 22 320
I J	+ 42 900	+ 76 200	± 19 200	+138 300
$k l$	− 9520	0	± 3200	− 12 720
$j k$	− 28 600	− 38 100	± 6400	− 73 100
$i j$	− 28 600	− 38 100	0	− 66 660

The work of erection cannot be safely

carried on at times when the wind blows at a high velocity, at which time the traveler should be run back to a point of safety. On this account no allowance has been made for stress in the members due to wind on the traveler placed in a position to effect the members given in the table.

Article 18.—Final Maximum and Minimum Stresses.

A table of stresses due to dead load, live load, snow load, and wind on truss is given for the cantilever bridge shown in Fig's VII and XIX, and the final maximum and minimum stresses given in the last two columns.

The overturning effect of wind on the truss has not been considered. It amounts to but little any way and would not change the final results much in this case. But in a through bridge it should be considered. Impact has been omitted because of its complication. Initial tension would enter into the final results of some of the members. All of these omitted forces are mentioned merely to call attention to them, so that the student may investigate the subject in works in which they are treated.

Attention is called to the final results, as showing in some members the reversal of stress from tension to compression and *visa versa.*

Table of Stresses in Highway Cantilever.

Member	Dead Load	Live Load	Snow Load	Wind on Truss E.	Wind on Truss W.	Maximum Stress	Minimum Stress
A B	+ 12 000	− 50 000 + 64 000	+ 4800	− 6000	0	+ 80 800	− 44 000
B C	+ 12 000	+ 50 000 − 64 000	+ 4800	− 17 000	+ 6000	+ 86 800	− 55 000
C D	+ 32 380	+ 57 140 + 121 900	+ 12 950	− 33 000	+ 17 000	+ 181 230	− 57 760
D E	+ 60 000	+ 54 545 + 174 540	+ 24 000	− 54 000	+ 33 000	+ 291 540	− 48 540
E F	+ 94 000	+ 34 800 + 222 610	+ 37 600	− 80 000	+ 54 000	+ 408 210	− 20 800
F G	+ 91 300	+ 182 600	+ 36 520	− 80 000	+ 52 500	+ 362 920	− 14 000
G H	+ 54 550	+ 109 090	+ 21 820	− 52 500	+ 30 000	+ 215 460	+ 2050
H I	+ 23 800	+ 47 620	+ 9520	− 30 000	+ 12 500	+ 93 440	− 6200
I J	+ 23 800	+ 47 620	+ 9520	− 12 500	0	+ 80 940	+ 11 300
J K	− 14 280	− 28 560 + 38 100	− 5710	0	− 6250	− 54 800	− 14 280
K L	− 19 050	+ 70 720	− 7620	− 6250	− 7500	− 72 270	− 12 800
A b	− 16 960	− 90 520 + 45 715	− 6785	− 4250	0	− 118 515	+ 53 760
b c	− 32 460	+ 91 430	− 12 985	− 8500	+ 3000	− 145 375	+ 16 255

Table of Stresses in Highway Cantilever—continued.

Member	Dead Load.	Live Load.	Snow Load.	Wind on Truss. E.	Wind on Truss. W.	Maximum Stress.	Minimum Stress.
c d	− 60 000	+ 32 730	− 24 000	− 16 500	+ 8500	− 225 935	− 18 770
d e	− 94 040	− 123 455	− 37 610	− 27 000	− 16 500	− 325 650	− 63 540
e f	− 133 600	+ 14 000	− 53 440	− 40 000	− 27 000	− 452 040	− 106 600
f g	− 133 500	− 167 000	− 53 400	− 40 000	− 26 250	− 493 900	− 107 250
g h	− 91 400	− 225 000	− 36 560	− 26 250	− 15 000	− 337 010	− 76 400
h i	− 54 600	− 267 000	− 21 840	− 15 000	− 6250	− 200 640	− 48 350
i J	− 34 530	− 182 800	− 13 810	− 8850	0	− 126 190	− 34 530
J k	+ 20 740	+ 109 000	+ 8300	0	− 5300	+ 70 240	+ 15 440
k l	+ 14 280	+ 41 200	+ 5710	+ 3750	− 5000	+ 52 300	+ 9280
B b	− 10 000	− 22 800	− 4000			− 36 800	− 10 000
b C	+ 28 820	+ 20 000	+ 11 530			+ 115 900	+ 28 820
C c	− 30 400	− 75 550	− 12 160			− 105 130	− 30 400
c D	+ 40 120	+ 62 570	+ 16 050			+ 138 810	+ 40 120
D d	− 39 000	− 81 640	− 15 600			− 127 420	− 39 000
d E	+ 50 450	+ 72 820	+ 20 180			+ 164 965	+ 50 450
E e	− 43 175	− 94 235	− 17 270			− 146 795	− 43 175
e F	+ 55 000	+ 110 000	+ 22 000			+ 187 000	+ 55 000

71

Table of Stresses in Highway Cantilever—continued.

Member	Dead Load.	Live Load.	Snow Load.	Wind on Truss. E.	Wind on Truss. W.	Maximum Stress.	Minimum Stress.
F f	− 99 900	− 199 625	− 39 960	− 70 200	+ 70 200	− 409 686	− 29 700
F y	+ 64 090	+ 128 180	+ 25 640			+ 217 910	+ 64 090
g G	− 50 440	− 100 880	− 20 175			− 171 495	− 50 440
G h	+ 54 700	+ 110 000	+ 21 880			+ 186 580	+ 54 700
h H	− 42 280	− 84 550	− 16 910			− 143 740	− 42 280
H i	+ 44 650	+ 89 390	+ 17 860			+ 151 890	+ 44 650
i I	− 10 000	− 20 000	− 4000			− 34 000	− 10 000
k K	− 15 000	− 30 000	− 6000			− 51 000	− 15 000
K l		− 20 740					
l L	+ 6900	+ 20 740	+ 2610			+ 30 250	− 13 840
	− 10 000	− 20 000	− 4000			− 34 000	− 10 000

————— COUNTERS. —————

B c	0	+ 31 600	0	0	0	0	0
C d	0	+ 14 710	0	0	0	0	0
D e	0	+ 4600	0	0	0	0	0

CHAPTER III.

RAILROAD CANTILEVER BRIDGES.

ARTICLE 19.—LOADS IN RAILROAD CANTILEVER BRIDGES.

In railroad bridges the loads causing stress in the members of the truss are dead, live and wind. Snow load is not considered, because it falls through between the ties.

The calculation of dead load has been fully discussed in Art. 4 for highway bridges, and the same remarks apply here.

The wind loads in railroad bridges differ considerably from those in highway bridges. In addition to the effect of wind blowing on the truss the wind blowing on the train is considered, both as regards its effect in stressing the lateral bracing, and in overturning the bridge and causing additional stress in the leeward truss members. The wind on the truss is considered as a moving load, and care should be taken to place the train in the same position that it occupied when live load stress was found, so that the stresses due to the different causes may be properly combined.

(For live load in railroad bridges, see Art. 22.)

ARTICLE 20. — REACTION DUE TO DEAD LOAD.

The stresses due to dead load in a railroad cantilever bridge are calculated in precisely the same way as for a highway cantilever of the same arrangement of members.

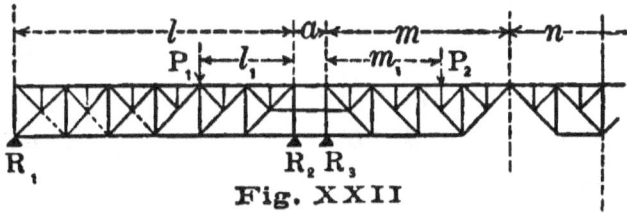

Fig. XXII

The railroad cantilever bridge used in the following analysis of stresses will be that shown in Fig. XXII.

It differs from those so far considered in that it has three points of support, R_1, R_2 and R_3, and the cantilever would therefore form a system in which the strains are ambiguous if the web system were continuous from end to end. If the diagonals in the panel between R_2 and R_3 are omitted, this ambiguity disappears, inasmuch as the strains transmitted by the remaining members of that panel are those due to moments, and the shear in the panel is zero.

The equations for reactions are found as follows:

Let P_1 be the resultant of all the loads on the shore arm, P_2 the resultant of all the loads on the river arm and central span, and let l_1 and m_1 be their respective distances from R_2 and R_3. The fundamental principle that the algebraic sum of the vertical forces shall equal zero, gives

$$R_1 + R_2 + R_3 - P_1 - P_2 = 0 \quad \ldots\ldots(16)$$

and since the shear in the panel between R_2 and R_3 is zero,

$$P_2 - R_3 = 0, \text{ or } R_3 = P_2 \ldots\ldots(17)$$

That is to say, R_s equals the load on the right of R_s; therefore

$$R_1 + R_2 = P_1 \quad \ldots\ldots\ldots\ldots(18)$$

The equation of moments of the external forces with reference to point at reaction, R_2, is

$$R_1 l - P_1 l_1 + P_2(a + m_1) - R_s a = 0,$$

but $R_s = P_2$ and the equation reduces to

$$R_1 = \frac{P_1 l_1 - P_2 m_1}{l} \quad \ldots\ldots\ldots\ldots(19)$$

The moment of forces with reference to point R_1 as origin, gives

$$P_1(l - l_1) + P_2(l + a + m_1) - R_2 l \\ - R_s(l + a) = 0 \ldots\ldots\ldots\ldots(20)$$

Substituting in equation (16) the values of R_s and R_1 as given in equations (17) and (19), gives

$$R_2 = \frac{P_1(l - l_1) + P_2 m_1}{l} \quad \ldots\ldots\ldots(21)$$

These equations are general for this class of cantilever, and may be used for both uniform and concentrated load, with slight modifications.

Article 21.—Stresses Due to Dead Load.

Let the single track deck railroad bridge shown in Fig. XXIII have the following dimensions: Length of shore arm 180 feet, river arm 120 feet and central span 120 feet; the panel length on the upper chord 15 feet, except the panel between R_2 and R_3, which is 10 feet; the depth of truss 30 feet and distance apart of trusses 16 feet.

Let the dead apex load on the upper chord be assumed at 12 000 pounds, and the apex load on the lower chord 4000 pounds.

The total dead load is then 356 000 pounds.

$P_2 = 172\ 000$ pounds, and $P_1 = 184\ 000$ pounds.

Taking a full apex load at A and a, the reactions are found to be as follows:

From (17), $R_3 = P_2 = 172\ 000$ pounds.

Equation (16) gives $R_1 + R_2 + R_3 = P_1 + P_2 = 356\ 000$ pounds.

From (18), $R_1 + R_2 = P_1 = 184\,000$ pounds and R_1 is found from (19) to be
$R_1 \times 180 = 184\,000 \times 90 - 108\,000 \times 60 - 16\,000 \times 45 - 48\,000 \times 120$,
or $R_1 = +20\,000$ pounds.
$R_2 = P_1 - R_1 = 184\,000 - 20\,000 = +164\,000$ pounds.

With the reactions known, the calculation of stress in the members of truss due to dead load is a comparatively simple matter. The members are arranged after the manner of the Baltimore truss with chords horizontal.

The angle θ which the inclined web members make with the vertical is 45 degrees, the secant of which is 1.41.

The stress in each sub-vertical $B\,b$, $D\,d$, $F\,f$, etc., is equal to the apex load that comes upon them, which in the case of dead load is 12 000 pounds.

All the members $A\,b$, $C\,d$, $E\,f$, Ts, Tu, etc., are stressed alike and equal to
$$\frac{12\,000}{2} \sec\theta, \text{ or}$$
$6000 \times 1.41 = 8460$ pounds.

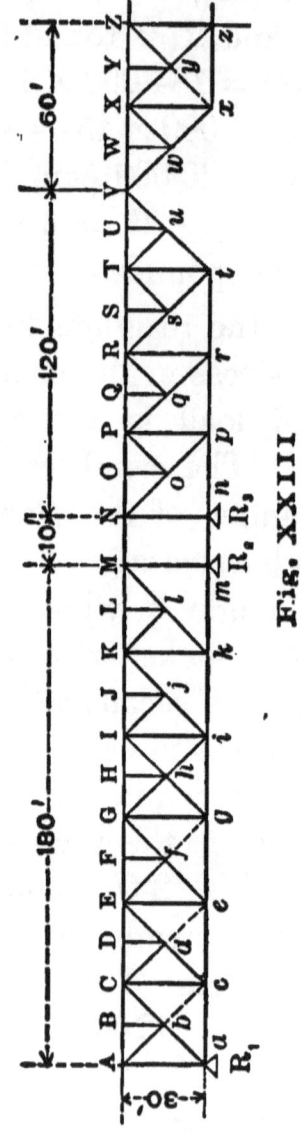

Fig. XXIII

To calculate the stress in ac, pass a section cutting three members BC, Cb and ac, then take the center of moments at C and equate the moment of the forces on the left of the section to zero,

$$ac \times 30 + (20\,000 - 16\,000)\,30$$
$$- 12\,000 \times 15 = 0,$$
$$\text{and } ac = -2000 \text{ pounds.}$$

For the member DE proceed in the same manner, taking the center of moments at c, the equation is

$$DE \times 30 + 4000 \times 30 - 12\,000 \times 15$$
$$+ 12\,000 \times 15 = 0 \text{ from}$$
$$\text{which } DE = -4000 \text{ pounds.}$$

The stress in Gf is found by multiplying the shear in the section cutting it, by $\sec\theta$.

$$\text{Shear} = 20\,000 - 3 \times 4000 - 6 \times 12\,000$$
$$= 64\,000$$

and $Gf = 64\,000 \times 1.41 = 90\,240$ pounds.

The stress in MN is found by taking the center of moments at n and expressing the moment of the forces on the right of the section, thus

$$MN \times 30 = 60\,000 \times 120 + 48\,000 \times 60$$
$$+ 48\,000 \times 60$$

or M N $= +$ 432 000 pounds.

From the fundamental condition of static equilibrium, namely, that the sum of the horizontal components of the stresses in any section must equal zero,
$$M N = mn = km = np.$$

In calculating the stresses for the members in the river arm it is best to consider the forces on the right of the section; for example, to find the stress in P Q, pass section cutting P Q, P q and pr. Take center of moments at r, and the moment of the forces on the right is made equal to P Q times its lever arm, or

$$P Q \times 30 = 60\ 000 \times 60 + 40\ 000 \times 30 \\ - 12\ 000 \times 15,$$

which gives P Q $= +$ 154 000 pounds.

Article 22.—Live Load.

The live load generally taken for calculation of stresses in the members of bridges in America, consists of two of the heaviest locomotives in general use, followed by a train load of about 3000 pounds per linear foot.

The exact solution of stresses due to such a live load for simple trusses is given in standard works on stresses in framed structures. The work involved in calculating the stresses due to the true-wheel load method is considerably greater than that required by the use of uniform train load with excess loads; and, since the locomotive load specified by different railroad companies varies considerably in different parts of the country, there arises on the part of bridge building companies a general desire for some conventional method of treating the train load which will give easy and short computations without giving results materially different from the true ones.

Very close approximations to the actual wheel loads have been found, and used quite extensively in bridge computation.

The one given and used by Prof. A. J. Dubois, in his "Framed Structures" involves the use of two concentrated excess loads placed 50 feet apart, either ahead of, or in the middle of a uniform train load, as desired, for max. shear and moments.

Another method, and one quite extensively used on account of its simplicity and satisfactory agreement with the wheel load method, was proposed by Geo. H. Pegram, in *Transactions Am. Soc. C. E.*, *for* 1886. This method makes use of one excess load, which may occupy any position in the uniform train load, and which may be conceived as rolling across the span on top of the uniform train load.

In the following analysis of stresses the live load is taken as consisting of a uniform train load and one concentrated excess load, except when the train is divided so as to occupy two different portions of the bridge, when an excess load may be taken with each part. This kind of loading is adopted because it is easier, and renders the analysis of stresses much simpler and more easily understood, while at the same time omitting none of the principles involved in the exact wheel-load method.

Article 23.—Live Load Stresses.

Assuming the excess load acting on one truss to be 20 000 pounds, and the uniform train load at 2000 pounds per foot or 2000 × 15 = 30 000 pounds apex load, the live load stresses for the cantilever of Fig. XXIII are found, as follows: Since the live load consists of uniform load and one excess load, the proper position of these loads to give maximum positive and negative shears and moments will be found by reference to the rules already established in Articles 11, 12, and 13.

The maximum live-load stress in Bb, Dd, etc., will occur when the uniform train panel load and excess load come upon them, and is 30 000 + 20 000 = 50 000 pounds.

Let the chord stresses be considered. In Arts. 11 and 13 it is shown that the chord members in the shore arm are subject to positive and negative bending moment, according to the position of the live load. Maximum positive moment, producing compression in upper and tension in lower chord, occurs when the uniform live load covers the entire shore arm, with the excess load at the center of moments.

Maximum negative moment, producing tension in upper chord and compression in lower chord occurs when the river arm and central span is loaded, with the excess load at the end of the river arm. The upper chord is always tension and lower chord always compression in river arm, and is a maximum for this particular kind of truss and arrangement of web members when the live load covers central span and that part of river arm to the right of origin of moments with the excess load placed at the end of the river arm.

The central span, being a simple truss, requires no discussion as to proper loading, since that is supposed to be understood.

The greatest tensile stress in *ac* due to live load will be produced by positive moment, or, when the uniform live load covers the shore arm and the excess load at the center of moments, which is at apex point C. The reaction R_1 for this position of

load, if half a uniform panel load is assumed to come at A, is $R_1 = \dfrac{30\,000 \times 13}{2}$
$- 15\,000 + \dfrac{5}{6} \times 20\,000 = 196\,666$ pounds.
and $ac \times 30 = (196\,666 - 15\,000)\,30 - 30\,000 \times 15 = +\,166\,666$ pounds.

This result is true if ab is allowed to take compression which it is not, because the counter bc comes into action thus reducing ac to o.

For F G the center of moments is at e and the excess load at E. The reaction R_1 is $180\,000 + \dfrac{4}{6} \times 20\,000 = 193\,334$ pounds.

Then $- FG = - EF =$
$\dfrac{(193\,334 - 15\,000)\,60 - 30\,000\,(45 + 30)}{30}$
and $FG = -\,281\,670$ pounds.

In order to find the stress in the chord members of the shore arm due to negative moment, the river arm and central span must be covered with the uniform train load, with the excess load at the end of the river arm.

The reaction R_1 due to this position of the load is equal to
$$\frac{(135\,000 + 20\,000)\,120 + 210\,000 \times 60}{180}$$
pounds, or $R_1 = -\,173\,333$ pounds.

To find maximum compressive stress in $c\,e$ pass section through $D\,E$, $E\,d$ and $c\,e$, and take the center of moments at E, then $c\,c = \dfrac{173\,333 \times 60}{30} = -\,346\,670$ pounds.

In the same manner
$$k\,m \times 30 = 173\,330 \times 6 \times 30$$
and $k\,m = m\,n = n\,p = -\,1\,040\,000$ pounds.

Let a few of the chord stresses in the river arm be next considered. Here the upper chord is always in tension and lower chord in compression.

Attention is called to the fact that a greater stress can be obtained in the upper chord members, if the central span and river arm is loaded with the uniform load on the right of the center of moments than if the load extends up to the section with the excess load in either case at the end of the river arm. This is proved by the two following equations representing the stress in P Q for the two conditions of loading alluded to:

Passing section through P Q, P q and $p\,r$ and taking center of moments at r, the equations of moments when load extends to section is P Q =
$$\frac{155\,000 \times 60 + 90\,000 \times 30 - 30\,000 \times 15}{30}$$
or P Q = + 385 000 pounds.

When the load is placed on the right of the origin of moments; that is, up to and including apex point S, the equation is
$$P\,Q = \frac{155\,000 \times 60 + 90\,000 \times 30}{30} = +$$
400 000 pounds.

This proves that the stress in P Q is 15 000 pounds greater when the load extends only as far as the middle of the panel to the right of the center of moments than when it is brought up to the section.

For the stress in $p\,r$ take the center of moments at P, then

$$pr = \frac{155\,000 \times 90 + 150\,000 \times 45}{30}$$

or $pr = -\,690\,000$ pounds.

The calculation of stresses in the web members of the river arm involves the very same principles of loading that were used in the calculation of web stresses in river arm of highway bridge, Art. 14.

Take, for example, the member $R\,s$. Its stress is equal to the shear in the section multiplied by 1.41.

The maximum shear will take place when all the load possible is put on the right of the section, or when the central span and river arm right of section is loaded with uniform load, and with excess load at some point between section and end of river arm.

The maximum shear in section is then 245 000 pounds, and

$R\,s = 245\,000 \times 1.41 = +\,345\,450$ pounds.

To find the stresses in the web members of the shore arm is the most troublesome part of the whole problem, but with care in placing the loads in the proper position to produce the greatest possible positive and negative shears, the stresses become readily known when R_1 is known.

Take, for example, the member E d. The greatest possible tensile stress in this member will occur when the river arm and central span is loaded with uniform load and with excess load at end of river arm and the shore arm covered left of section.

The reaction R_1 due to this loading is from formula (19), $R_1 =$

$$\frac{155\,000 \times 120 + 210\,000 \times 60 - 90\,000 \times 150}{180}$$

$= -\,98\,335.$

The shear in section is then $-\,98\,335\,-\,90\,000 = 188\,355$ and

E $d = 188\,335 \times 1.41 = +\,265\,550$ pounds.

This result is obtained on a rather rediculous supposition, in that the load on left of the the section on shore arm, though isolated from the other load on river arm, is assumed to come into the desired position without any locomotive or excess load to place it there. A more reasonable supposition would be to place an excess load at the head of the uniform load left of the section on shore arm.

Finding R_1 by means of formula (19) gives,

$- R_1 \times 180 = 155\,000 \times 120 + 210\,000 \times 60 + 90\,000 \times 150 - 20\,000 \times 135$, and $R_1 = -83\,335$ pounds.

The shear in section is $-83\,335 - 110\,000 = -193\,335$ and $E\,d = 193\,335 \times 1.41 = +272\,600$ pounds.

The stress $c\,d$ is equal to the stress in $E\,d$ minus the stress in $E\,d$ caused by the apex load at D or $c\,d = 272\,600 - 35\,250 = +237\,350$ pounds.

Since $c\,d$ supports $C\,c$ the stress in $C\,c$ must equal the vertical component of the stress in $c\,d$; therefore $C\,c$ equals $237\,350 \div 1.41$.

or $C\,c = -168\,330$ pounds.

The stress in $N\,n = R_3 = P_2 = -395\,000$ pounds, and $M\,m$ equals R_2, but from formula (18), $R_2 = P_1 - R_1$.

The greatest value for R_2 will occur when the bridge is covered with live load. That on the river arm and central span being in the position occupied for maxi-

mum negative moment in shore arm, while the shore arm is covered with uniform live load with excess load at M. This gives
$P_1 = -(12 \times 30\,000 + 20\,000 + 15\,000) = -395\,000$ pounds, and
$R_1 \times 180 = 155\,000 \times 120 + 210\,000 \times 60 - (11 \times 30\,000)\,90 - 15\,000 \times 180$
or $R_1 = +6666$ pounds, and
$R_2 = M\,m = -395\,000 - 6666 = 401\,666$ pounds.

The maximum negative live load stress in $c\,d$ and $d\,E$ is produced when the shore arm is loaded on the right of a section cutting D E, d E and $c\,e$ with the excess load at E. R_1 due to this position of the load is
$$R_1 = \left(\tfrac{1}{12}+\tfrac{2}{12}+\tfrac{3}{12}\ldots\ldots\tfrac{8}{12}\right)30\,000 + \tfrac{2}{3}\times 20\,000 = 103\,335$$
and $c\,d = d\,E = 103\,335 \times 1.41 = -145\,700$ pounds.

Here is a member which shows itself to be subject to alternate tension and compression for different positions of the live load, which is an objectionable condition, and can be avoided by the introduction of a counter member $d\,c$, which will prevent the members cd and $d\,E$ from taking compression.

The actual effective compressive stress that can occur in cd, is the algebraic sum of the stresses in cd due to dead live and wind on train loads, which, taken from the table of stress are $+$ 42 300 $-$ 145 700 and $-$11 320 respectively, the sum of which is $-$ 114 720 pounds.

This is very nearly the value of the stress in the counter de. A counter is needed, therefore, in any panel in which the live load and wind overturning load negative shear exceeds numerically the dead-load positive shear. By reference to the table of final maximum and minimum stresses, it is readily seen that the only panels which need counter bracing are the first three at the end of the shore arm or bc, de and fg. In practice another panel might be counter braced for the sake of security.

ARTICLE 25.—WIND LOAD STRESSES.

Wind blowing on a bridge produces a

double effect. First,—it has the effect of stressing the members of the lateral system, and thereby producing compression in the windward chords and tension in the leeward chords. Second,—it has the effect of overturning the bridge. This latter effect produces an additional vertical load on the leeward truss, and consequently greater stress in the members of it, while at the same time decreasing the stress in the members of the windward truss. The change of stress in web members of trusses due to overturning effect of wind is caused, however, by the wind on train or live load alone, while the chord members are effected by both wind on train and wind on truss.

Let the wind apex load on both the upper and lower chords due to wind on truss be 2000 pounds, except the end apex load, which is 1000 pounds.

The stresses in the lateral system and chord members are now found by applying the principles given in the case of highway bridge, Art. 16. The reactions

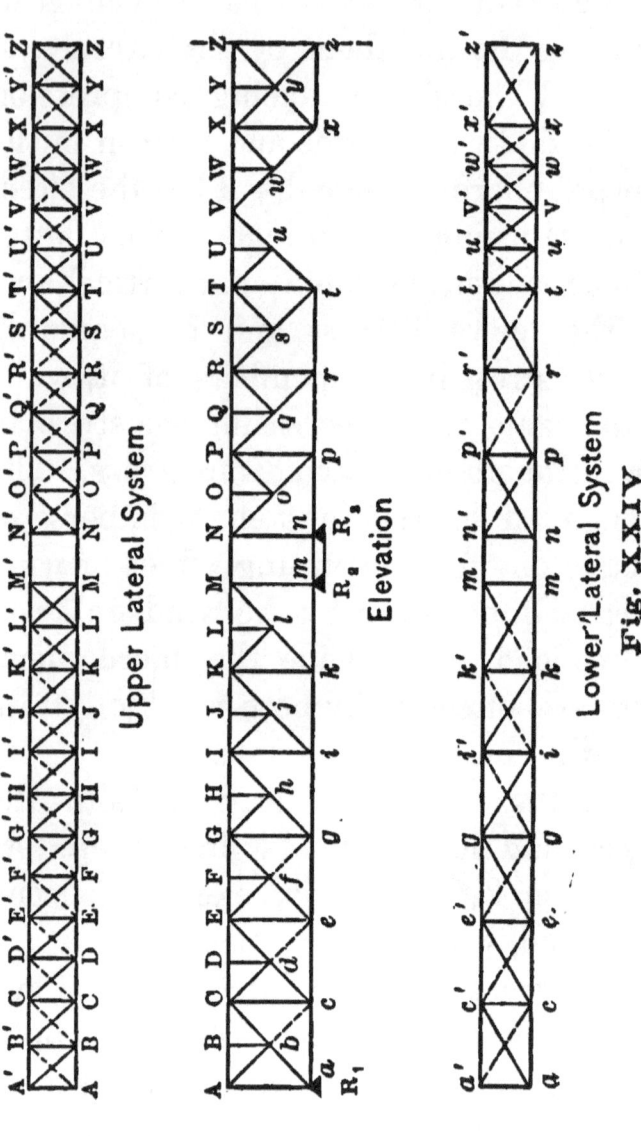

Fig. XXIV

are found by reference to Fig. XXIV, to be as follows:

For the upper lateral system from formula (18), $R_s = + 56\,000$, and for lower lateral system $R_s = + 16\,000$ pounds. From formula (19), R_1 for upper and lower lateral system equals $- 3333$ and $+ 8000$ pounds respectively. These results are obtained on the supposition that the wind apex loads on the central span are all transmitted by the lateral systems of the central span to the end of the river arm, and then acts through the lateral system of the upper chord. This is a rather more reasonable supposition than that in the case of wind in the highway bridge of Art. 16, where the wind apex loads on the lower chord of the central span were assumed to be transmitted to the end of the river arm, and then into the lower chord of the river arm by means of the inclined transverse bracing $J\,i'$ and $J'\,i$. See Fig. XIX.

R_s for upper system is found from formula (21) to be $+ 53\,333$ pounds, and for lower system $+ 18\,000$ pounds. To find the stress in any web member of the upper lateral system due to wind on truss, multiply the shear into the secant of the angle which the member makes with the vertical. For N O' shear is 52 000 pounds, and $\mathrm{Sec}\theta = \frac{22}{16} = 1.4$, and N O' = 52 000 × 1.4 = + 72 800 pounds.

The same stress takes effect in N' O when wind is reversed. Since these members are duplicates the stress is given for only one system. Stress in P P' is simply the shear or P P' = — 46 000 pounds.

The overturning effect of wind on the truss is, in the case of a cantilever bridge, a doubtful quantity, and very difficult of satisfactory determination. It is perfectly evident in the problem at hand that the wind blowing on the shore arm affects the chord stresses in connection with the lateral bracing, and that this effect is transmitted by the lateral system to the ends of the shore arm, where, by means of the cross-frame it is transmitted directly to the abutment and pier. The wind on the river arm and central span, or that part of it acting on the lower chord, has, however, the effect of twisting the river arm, and thereby causing some additional stress to the chord members of the central span, as well as additional stress in both chord and web members of the river arm. This change of stress must take place either when the train is on the bridge or when the bridge is unloaded. In the first case the overturning effect of wind on train would have the opposite effect to the wind on truss; or, in other words, would counteract the overturning effect of wind on truss. In the second case, the wind blowing at a time when no train is on the bridge, the overturning effect of which on truss would give stresses which combined with the dead-load stresses would give results very much less than the possible maximum stresses caused when the bridge is loaded. For these reasons the stresses in the members of truss due to the overturning effect of wind on the truss will be omitted.

The overturning effect of wind on the train, however, gives additional stresses in members of the truss, which, acting at the time when the live load acts, should be taken into account to give the maximum stresses. Assume the train to consist of box cars 10 feet high, and the wind pressure per square foot 30 pounds. This gives 300 pounds per linear foot, or $300 \times 15 = 4500$ pounds per panel. Taking the center of pressure of the wind at 9.5 feet above the center of the upper chord, the overturning moment at each panel point is then $4500 \times 9.5 = 42\,750$ pounds. This causes an additional vertical weight to act at each apex point of the leeward girder, equal to $42\,750 \div 16 = 2675$ pounds, and relieves the windward girder by the same amount.

This apex load effects the chord and web members of the truss in the same manner as a live apex load, and the process of finding the stress is consequently a repetition of that for live load.

Since the final maximum and minimum stresses are the result of combining those stresses caused by the different possible loading, it is necessary that care should be taken to get the stress in the members due to overturning effect of wind, when the live load occupies the same position on the bridge that it occupied when the live-load stresses were calculated.

The stress in the members of the cross frames of the bridge have not been calculated, since the method of calculating them has been explained at the end of Article 16, in highway bridges, and differs in the railroad bridge only in the additional surface exposed to the wind by the train, or 4500 pounds per panel.

This force is to be considered only when the bridge is a deck structure, since the wind on the train is transmitted through the wheels and track to the chord on which it rests.

Section of Truss and Train with Forces and Lever Arms.

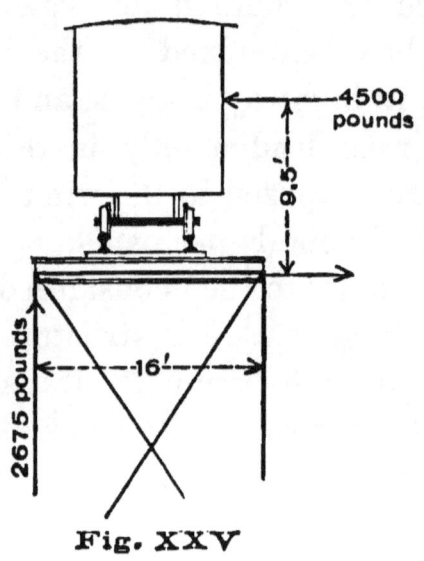

Fig. XXV

Wind Stresses in Lateral Systems of Fig. XXIV.

Member.	Wind on Truss.	Wind on Train.	Maximum Stress.	Member.	Wind on Truss.	Wind on Train.	Maximum Stress.
Z Z'	− 2000	− 5625	− 7625	P P'	− 46 000	− 47 250	− 93 250
Y Z'	+ 2800	+ 7875	+ 10 675	O P'	+ 67 200	+ 66 150	+ 133 350
Y Y'	− 4000	− 8440	− 12 440	O O'	− 50 000	− 51 750	− 101 750
X Y'	+ 8440	+ 11 816	+ 20 216	N O'	+ 72 800	+ 72 450	+ 145 250
X X'	− 8000	− 11 812	− 19 812	N N'	− 54 000	− 56 250	− 110 250
W X'	+ 14 000	+ 16 536	+ 30 536	z x'	− 2000		
W W'	− 12 000	− 15 750	− 27 750	x x'	+ 2160		
V W'	+ 19 600	+ 22 050	+ 41 650	w x'	− 4000	No Stresses on Lower La'eral	Maximum Stress same as
V V'	− 22 000	− 20 250	− 42 250	w w'	+ 9960	System due to wind on train.	wind on truss.
U V'	+ 33 600	+ 28 350	+ 61 950	V w'	− 6000		
U U'	− 26 000	− 24 750	− 50 750	t t'	+ 9960		
T U'	+ 30 200	+ 33 750	+ 72 950	r t'	− 2000		
T T'	− 30 000	− 29 250	− 59 250	p r'	+ 8480		
S T'	+ 44 800	+ 40 950	+ 85 750	p p'	− 6000		
S S'	− 34 000	− 33 750	− 67 750	n p'	+ 16 960		
R S'	+ 50 400	+ 47 250	+ 97 650	n n'	− 10 000		
R R'	− 38 000	− 38 250	− 76 250	m m'	+ 25 440		
Q R'	+ 56 000	+ 53 550	+ 109 550	m k'	− 14 000		
Q Q'	− 42 000	− 42 750	− 84 750		− 16 000		
P Q'	+ 61 600	+ 59 850	+ 121 450		+ 29 680		

Wind Stresses in Lateral Systems of Fig. XXIV.

Member	Wind on Truss.	Wind on Train.	Maximum Stress. (Maximum Stress same as wind on truss. No stress s due to wind on train.)	Member	Wind on Truss.	Wind on Train.	Maximum Stress.
k k'	− 12 000			E' F	+ 29 860	+ 38 850	+ 68 710
k i'	+ 21 200			F' F	− 23 330	− 29 625	− 52 955
i i'	− 8000			F' G	+ 35 460	+ 41 475	+ 76 935
i g'	+ 12 720			G' G	− 27 330	− 31 875	− 59 205
g g'	− 4000			G' H	+ 41 060	+ 44 065	+ 85 685
g e'	+ 4240			H' H	− 31 330	− 34 500	− 65 830
e e'	− 2000			H' I	+ 46 660	+ 48 300	+ 94 960
c e'	+ 4240			I' I	− 35 330	− 37 500	− 72 830
c c'	− 4000			I' J	+ 52 260	+ 52 500	+ 104 760
a c'	+ 12 720			J' J	− 39 330	− 40 875	− 80 205
a a'	− 7000			J' K	+ 57 860	+ 57 225	+ 115 085
A' A	+ 4330	− 26 250	− 30 580	K' K	− 43 330	− 44 625	− 87 955
A' B	+ 7460	+ 34 650	+ 42 110	K' L	+ 63 460	+ 62 475	+ 125 935
B' B	− 7330	− 24 375	− 31 705	L' L	− 47 330	− 48 750	− 96 080
B' C	+ 13 060	+ 34 125	+ 47 185	L' M	+ 69 060	+ 68 250	+ 137 310
C' C	− 11 330	− 25 125	− 36 455	M' M	− 51 330	− 53 250	− 104 680
C' D	+ 18 660	+ 35 175	+ 53 835				
D' D	− 15 330	− 26 250	− 41 580				
D' E	+ 24 260	+ 36 750	+ 61 010				
E' E	− 19 330	− 27 750	− 47 080				

Stresses for R. R. Cantilever shown in Fig. XXIII.

Member.	Dead Load.	Live Load.	Wind Overturning on Train.		Maximum Stress.	Minimum Stress.
			E.	W.		
A a	− 12 000	− 198 300	− 16 050	+ 16 050	− 226 350	− 12 000
B b	− 12 000	− 50 000	− 2675	+ 2675	− 64 675	− 12 000
C c	− 24 000	− 168 330	− 12 710	+ 12 710	− 205 040	− 24 000
D d	− 12 000	− 50 000	− 2675	+ 2675	− 64 675	− 12 000
E e	− 54 000	− 194 170	− 15 000	+ 15 000	− 263 170	− 54 000
F f	− 12 000	− 50 000	− 2675	+ 2675	− 64 675	− 12 000
G g	− 82 000	− 229 670	− 17 210	+ 17 210	− 328 880	− 82 000
H h	− 12 000	− 50 000	− 2675	+ 2675	− 64 675	− 12 000
I i	− 110 000	− 275 835	− 22 070	+ 22 070	− 407 905	− 110 000
J j	− 12 000	− 50 000	− 2675	+ 2675	− 64 675	− 12 000
K k	− 138 000	− 331 670	− 27 630	+ 27 630	− 497 300	− 138 000
L l	− 12 000	− 50 000	− 2675	+ 2675	− 64 675	− 12 000
M m	− 160 000	− 401 660	− 34 640	+ 31 640	− 596 300	− 160 000
N n	− 168 000	− 395 000	− 33 440	+ 33 440	− 596 440	− 168 000
O o	− 12 000	− 50 000	− 2675	+ 2675	− 64 675	− 12 000
P p	− 146 000	− 365 000	− 29 425	+ 29 425	− 540 425	− 146 000
Q q	− 12 000	− 50 000	− 2675	+ 2675	− 64 675	− 12 000
R r	− 118 000	− 305 000	− 24 075	+ 24 075	− 447 075	− 118 000
S s	− 12 000	− 50 000	− 2675	+ 2675	− 64 675	− 12 000
T t	− 24 000	− 80 000	− 5350	+ 5350	− 109 350	− 24 000
U u	− 12 000	− 50 000	− 2675	+ 2675	− 64 675	− 12 000

Stresses for R. R. Cantilever shown in Fig. XXIII.

Member	Dead Load	Live Load	Wind on Truss		Wind on Train		Overturning Effect of Wind on Train.		Maximum Stress.	Minimum Stress.
			E.	W.	E.	W.	E.	W.		
W w	− 12 500	− 50 000				0		− 2675	− 64 675	− 12 000
X x	− 38 000	− 71 250				− 48 400		− 8025	− 117 275	− 38 000
Y y	− 12 000	− 50 000						− 2675	− 64 675	− 12 000
Z z	− 24 000	− 80 000						− 5350	− 109 350	− 24 000
A B	− 6000	− 154 350	− 3125		− 22 500	0	− 12 260	− 12 260	− 198 235	− 6000
B C	− 6000	− 154 350	− 10 000	+ 3125	− 23 200	+ 22 500	− 12 260	+ 12 260	− 159 410	− 2875
C D	− 4000	+ 173 330	− 20 625	+ 10 000	− 45 000	+ 57 000	− 3345	+ 3345	+ 161 200	+ 110 050
		− 181 670			− 48 440	+ 45 000	− 14 270	+ 14 270		
D E	− 4000	+ 173 330	− 35 000	+ 20 625	− 67 500	+ 67 500	− 3345	+ 3345	+ 243 185	+ 167 015
		− 281 670			− 57 000	+ 67 500	− 14 270	+ 14 270		
E F	+ 26 000	+ 346 670	− 53 120	+ 35 000	− 90 000	+ 73 830	− 28 535	+ 28 535	+ 469 135	+ 256 615
		− 281 670			− 67 500	+ 90 000	− 5325	+ 5325		
F G	+ 26 000	+ 346 670	− 75 000	+ 53 120	− 112 500	+ 77 200	− 28 535	+ 28 535	+ 509 085	+ 262 165
		− 300 000			− 73 830	+ 112 500	− 5325	+ 5325		
G H	+ 84 000	+ 520 000	− 100 620	+ 75 000	− 135 000	+ 77 200	− 6020	+ 6020	+ 761 200	+ 248 810
		− 300 000			− 73 380	+ 135 000	− 42 800	+ 42 800		
H I	+ 84 000	+ 520 000	− 130 000	+ 100 620	− 157 500	+ 73 830	− 5325	+ 5325	+ 819 320	+ 283 825
		− 266 670			− 67 500	+ 157 500	− 42 800	+ 42 800		
I J	+ 122 000	+ 693 330	− 163 120	+ 130 000	− 180 000	+ 67 500	− 5325	+ 5325	+ 1 068 260	+ 256 115
					− 202 500	+ 180 000	− 57 070	+ 57 070		

195

Stresses for R. R. Cantilever shown in Fig. XXIII.

Member.	Dead Load.	Live Load	Wind on Truss.		Wind on Train.		Overturning Effect of Wind on Train.		Maximum Stress.	Minimum Stress.
			E.	W.	E.	W.	E.	W.		
J K	+122 000	+266 670 / +693 330	−200 000	+163 120	+48 440 / −225 000	−57 000 / +202 500	+57 070	−57 070	+1 123 880	−296 230
K L	+284 000	+166 670 / +866 670	−240 620	+200 000	+23 200 / −247 500	−48 440 / +225 000	+71 340	−71 340	+1 504 330	−100 090
L M	+284 000	+166 670 / +866 670	−285 000	+240 620	0 / −270 000	−23 200 / +247 500	+71 340	−71 340	+1 567 450	−157 670
M N	+432 000	−1 040 000	−285 000	+285 000	−270 000	−270 000	+85 605	−85 605	+1 941 400	+147 000
N O	+260 000	+690 000	−285 000	+236 250	−270 000	−221 485	+56 175	−56 175	+1 351 560	+25 000
O P	+260 000	+690 000	−236 250	+191 250	−221 485	−177 190	+56 175	−56 175	+1 262 315	+24 000
P Q	+154 000	+400 000	−191 250	+150 000	−177 190	−137 110	+32 100	−32 100	+809 010	+37 250
Q R	+154 000	+400 000	−150 000	+112 500	−137 100	−101 250	+32 100	−32 100	+735 650	+4 000
R S	+60 000	+170 000	−111 500	+78 750	−101 250	−70 000	+13 400	−13 400	+365 360	+51 540
S T	+60 000	+170 000	−78 750	+48 750	−70 000	−42 200	+3 400	−13 400	+307 550	+18 750
T U	+60 000	+155 000	−48 750	+22 500	−42 200	−19 000	+2 040	−12 040	+256 500	+11 250
U V	+60 000	+155 000	−22 500	0	−19 000	0	+12 040	−12 040	+227 040	+30 540
V W	+48 000	+122 500	0	+13 125	0	+14 770	−9360	−9360	+189 085	+48 000
W X	+48 000	+122 500	+13 125	−22 500	+14 770	−25 300	−9360	−9360	+208 940	+34 875
X Y	−14 000	−115 000	+22 500	−28 250	+25 300	−21 700	−16 050	+16 050	−172 900	−9500
Y Z	−14 000	−115 000	+28 250	−30 000	+31 700	−33 750	−16 050	+16 050	−176 700	−14 250
a c	0	+174 670 / 0	0	−11 250			−14 270 / +13 375	+14 270 / −13 375	−185 920	0

Stresses for R. R. Cantilever shown in Fig. XXIII.

Member.	Dead Load.	Live Load.	Wind on Truss.		Wind on Train.		Overturning Effect of Wind on Train.		Maximum Stress.	Minimum Stress.
			E.	W.	E.	W.	E.	W.		
c e	− 32 000	+ 346 670					− 26 535	+ 28 535	+ 395 955	+266 650
		+ 266 000	+ 11 250	− 15 000			+ 21 400	− 21 400		
e g	− 90 000	− 520 000					− 42 800	+ 42 800		
		+ 300 000	+ 15 000	− 15 000			+ 24 075	− 24 075	+ 637 800	+249 075
g i	−176 000	− 693 330					− 57 070	+ 57 070		
		+ 266 670	+ 11 250	− 11 250			+ 21 400	− 21 400	+ 915 150	+123 320
i k	−290 000	+ 866 670					− 71 460	+ 71 460		
		− 166 670	− 18 750	0			+ 13 370	− 13 570	−1 246 890	−123 320
k m	−432 000	−1 040 000	− 45 000	+ 18 750			− 85 605	+ 85 605	−1 602 605	−327 645
m n	−432 000	−1 040 000	− 45 000	+ 45 000			+ 85 605	− 85 605	−1 602 605	−301 395
n p	−432 000	−1 040 000	− 45 000	+ 22 500			+ 85 605	− 85 605	−1 602 605	−323 895
p r	−282 000	− 690 000	− 22 500	+ 7500			− 56 175	+ 56 175	−1 050 675	−218 325
r t	−160 000	− 400 000	− 7500	0			− 32 100	+ 32 100	− 599 600	−127 900
x z	+ 42 000	+ 105 000	− 3750	+ 3750			−10 900	+10 900	+ 161 650	+ 27 350

107

Stresses for R. R. Cantilever shown in Fig. XXIII.

Member.	Dead Load.	Live Load.	Overturning Effect of Wind on Train.		Maximum Stress.	Minimum Stress.
			E.	W.		
A b	+ 2820 + 8460	+ 258 500 − 217 375	+ 20 750 − 17 290	− 20 750 + 17 290	+ 290 530	+ 11 280
O b	+ 8460	+ 250 280 − 217 375	+ 20 730 − 17 290	− 20 730 + 17 290	+ 279 470	+ 8460
a b / C d	+ 2820 + 8460	+ 125 140 ++ 179 775	+ 18 845 − 14 150	− 18 845 − 14 150	++ 141 165 ++ 202 385	0 + 8460
E d	+ 50 760	+ 272 600 − 145 700	+ 19 810 + 11 320	− 19 810 + 11 320	+ 343 170	+ 8460
c d / E f	+ 42 300 + 8460	+ 237 350 ++ 145 700	+ 17 925 − 11 320	− 17 925 + 11 320	++ 297 575 ++ 132 810	0 + 8460
G f	+ 90 240	++ 115 150 − 302 360	++ 8800 − 22 955	− 8800 − 22 955	+ 415 555	+ 8460
e f / G h	+ 81 780 + 8460	+ 88 125 ++ 267 110	+ 6600 + 21 070	− 6600 + 21 070	++ 369 960 ++ 48 425	0 + 8460
I h	+ 129 720	+ 88 125 ++ 35 250	+ 6600 + 4715	− 6600 + 4715	+ 516 300	+ 82 020
g h / I j	++ 121 260 ++ 8460	++ 359 550 − 44 650	++ 27 030 + 3150	− 27 030 + 3150	++ 470 685 ++ 45 595	+ 73 460 + 8460
K j / i j	++ 169 200 ++ 160 740	++ 324 300 − 44 600	++ 25 125 + 3150	− 25 125 + 3150	++ 626 380 ++ 587 445	+ 169 200 + 160 740
K l / M l	++ 8460 ++ 208 680	++ 35 250 ++ 424 180 ++ 395 590 ++ 35 250 ++ 503 500	++ 1885 ++ 33 000 ++ 31 115 − 1685 − 40 840	− 1885 − 33 000 − 31 115 − 1685 − 40 840	++ 45 595 ++ 753 020	+ 8460 + 208 680

108

Stresses for R. R. Cantilever shown in Fig. XXIII.

Member.	Dead Load.	Live Load.	Overturning Effect of Wind on Train.		Maximum Stress.	Minimum Stress.
			E.	W.		
k l	+ 200 220	+ 467 650	+ 38 955	− 38 955	+ 706 825	+ 200 220
N o	+ 219 960	+ 514 650	+ 43 375	− 43 375	+ 777 985	+ 219 960
P o	+ 8460	+ 35 250	+ 1885	− 1885	+ 45 595	+ 8460
p o	+ 211 500	+ 479 400	+ 41 490	− 41 490	+ 732 390	+ 215 500
P q	+ 180 480	+ 430 050	+ 31 835	− 31 835	+ 642 365	+ 180 480
R q	+ 8460	+ 35 250	+ 1885	− 1885	+ 45 600	+ 8460
r q	+ 172 000	+ 394 870	+ 33 950	− 33 950	+ 600 820	+ 162 000
R s	+ 141 000	+ 345 450	+ 28 400	− 28 400	+ 514 850	+ 141 000
T s	+ 8460	+ 35 250	+ 1885	− 1885	+ 45 600	+ 8460
t s	+ 132 540	+ 345 450	+ 26 410	− 26 410	+ 504 400	+ 132 540
T u	+ 8460	+ 35 250	+ 1885	− 1885	+ 45 600	+ 8460
V u	− 84 600	− 218 550	− 16 970	+ 16 970	− 320 120	− 84 600
t u	− 93 060	− 253 800	− 18 855	+ 18 855	− 465 715	− 93 060
V w	+ 67 680	+ 172 725	+ 13 180	− 13 180	+ 253 585	+ 67 680
X w	+ 8460	+ 35 250	+ 1885	− 1885	+ 45 600	+ 8460
x w	+ 59 220	+ 137 475	+ 11 295	− 11 295	+ 207 990	+ 59 220
X y	+ 28 000	− 22 910	− 1100	+ 1100	+ 130 590	+ 3990
		+ 96 930	+ 5660	− 5660		
		+ 42 300				
Z y	+ 8460	+ 35 250	+ 1885	− 1885	+ 45 600	+ 8460
z y	+ 19 740	+ 61 690	+ 3770	− 3770	+ 85 200	+ 19 740
COUNTERS.						
b c	+ 2820	+ 223 250	+ 18 870	− 18 870	+ 244 940	0
d e	− 42 300	− 144 530	− 12 265	+ 12 265	− 114 495	0
f g	− 81 780	− 79 900	− 6920	+ 6920	− 5040	0

CATALOGUE

OF THE

SCIENTIFIC PUBLICATION

OF

D. VAN NOSTRAND COMPANY,

23 Murray Street and 27 Warren Street, N. Y.

ADAMS (J. W.) Sewers and Drains for Populous Districts. 8vo, cloth............................ $2 50

ALEXANDER (J. H.) Universal Dictionary of Weights and Measures. 8vo, cloth 3 50

—— (S. A.) Broke Down: What Should I Do? A Ready Reference and Key to Locomotive Engineers and Firemen, Round-house Machinists, Conductors, Train Hands and Inspectors. With 5 folding plates. 12mo, cloth 1 50

ATKINSON (PHILIP). The Elements of Electric Lighting, including Electric Generation, Measurements, Storage, and Distribution. Seventh edition. Illustrated. 12mo, cloth........................... 1 50

—— The Elements of Dynamic Electricity and Magnetism. 120 illustrations. 12mo, cloth............... 2 00

—— Elements of Static Electricity, with full description of the Holtz and Topler Machines, and their mode of operating. Illustrated. 12mo, cloth 1 50

—— The Electric Transformation of Power and its Application by the Electric Motor, including Electric Railway Construction. Illustrated. 12mo, cloth...... 2 00

AUCHINCLOSS (W. S.) Link and Valve Motions Simplified. Illustrated with 37 woodcuts and 21 lithographic plates, together with a Travel Scale, and numerous useful tables. Eleventh edition. 8vo, cloth 3 00

BACON (F. W.) A Treatise on the Richards Steam-Engine Indicator, with directions for its use. By Charles T. Porter. Revised. Illustrated. 12mo, cloth....... 1 00

BADT (F. B.) Dynamo Tender's Hand-book. With 70 illustrations. Second edition. 18mo, cloth.......... 1 00

—— Bell-hangers' Hand-book. With 97 illustrations. 18mo, cloth.. 1 00

—— Incandescent Wiring Hand-book. With 35 illustrations and five tables. 18mo, cloth................. 1 00

—— Electric Transmission Hand-book. With 22 illustrations and 27 tables. 18mo, cloth................ 1 00

BALE (M. P.) Pumps and Pumping. A Hand-book for Pump Users. 12mo, cloth...................... 1 00

BARBA (J.) The Use of Steel for Constructive Purposes. Method of Working, Applying, and Testing Plates and Bars. With a Preface by A. L. Holley, C.E. 12mo, cloth 1 50

BARNARD (F. A. P.) Report on Machinery and Processes of the Industrial Arts and Apparatus of the Exact Sciences at the Paris Universal Exposition, 1867. 152 illustrations and 8 folding plates. 8vo, cloth... 5 00

BEAUMONT (ROBERT). Color in Woven Design. With 32 colored Plates and numerous original illustrations. Large 12mo.............................. 7 50

BEILSTEIN (F.) An Introduction to Qualitative Chemical Analysis. Translated by J. J. Osbun. 12mo cloth....

BECKWITH (ARTHUR). Pottery. Observations on the Materials and Manufacture of Terra-Cotta, Stoneware, Fire-brick, Porcelain, Earthenware, Brick, Majolica, and Encaustic Tiles. 8vo, paper........ 60

BERNTHSEN (A.) A Text-book of Organic Chemistry. Translated by George McGowan, Ph.D. 544 pages. Illustrated. 12mo, cloth 2 50

BIGGS (C. H. W.) First Principles of Electrical Engineering. 12mo, cloth. Illustrated............... 1 00

SCIENTIFIC PUBLICATIONS. 3

BLAKE (W. P.) Report upon the Precious Metals. 8vo, cloth 2 00

——— Ceramic Art. A Report on Pottery, Porcelain, Tiles, Terra-Cotta, and Brick. 8vo, cloth 2 00

BLAKESLEY (T. H.) Alternating Currents of Electricity. For the use of Students and Engineers. 12mo, cloth 1 50

BLYTH (A. WYNTER, M.R.C.S., F.C.S.) Foods: their Compositions and Analysis. Crown 8vo, cloth. ... 6 00

——— Poisons: their Effects and Detection. Crown 8vo, cloth 6 00

BODMER (G. R.) Hydraulic Motors; Turbines and Pressure Engines, for the use of Engineers, Manufacturers, and Students. With numerous illustrations. 12mo, cloth................................... 5 00

BOTTONE (S. R.) Electrical Instrument Making for Amateurs. With 48 illustrations. 12mo, cloth 50

——— Electric Bells, and all about them. Illustrated. 12mo, cloth 50

——— The Dynamo: How Made and How Used. 12mo, cloth.. 1 00

——— Electro Motors: How Made and How Used. 12mo. cloth.. 50

BONNEY (G. E.) The Electro-Platers' Hand-book. 60 Illustrations. 12mo, cloth.......................... 1 20

BOW (R. H.) A Treatise on Bracing. With its application to Bridges and other Structures of Wood or Iron. 156 illustrations. 8vo, cloth................. 1 50

BOWSER (Prof. E. A.) An Elementary Treatise on Analytic Geometry. Embracing plain Geometry, and an Introduction to Geometry of three Dimensions. 12mo, cloth. Thirteenth edition.................... 1 75

——— An Elementary Treatise on the Differential and Integral Calculus. With numerous examples. 12mo, cloth. Twelfth edition 2 25

——— An Elementary Treatise on Analytic Mechanics. With numerous examples. 12mo, cloth. Fifth edition. 3 00

BOWSER (Prof. E. A.) An Elementary Treatise on Hydro-mechanics. With numerous examples. 12mo, cloth. Third edition.................. .... 2 50

BOWIE (AUG. J., Jun., M. E.) A Practical Treatise on Hydraulic Mining in California. With Description of the Use and Construction of Ditches, Flumes, Wrought-iron Pipes, and Dams; Flow of Water on Heavy Grades, and its Applicability, under High Pressure, to Mining. Third edition. Small quarto, cloth. Illustrated........ .... 5 00

BURGH (N. P.) Modern Marine Engineering, applied to Paddle and Screw Propulsion. Consisting of 36 colored plates, 259 practical woodcut illustrations, and 403 pages of descriptive matter. Thick 4to vol., half morocco... ....10 00

BURT (W. A.) Key to the Solar Compass, and Surveyor's Companion. Comprising all the rules necessary for use in the field. Pocket-book form, tuck......... ..... 2 50

CALDWELL (Prof. GEO. C., and BRENEMAN (Prof. A. A.) Manual of Introductory Chemical Practice. 8vo, cloth. Illustrated......... .. ..,.......... 1 50

CAMPIN (FRANCIS). On the Construction of Iron Roofs. A Theoretical and Practical Treatise, with wood-cuts and plates of Roofs recently executed. 8vo, cloth........... .... 2 00

CLEEMAN (THOS. M.) The Railroad Engineer's Practice. Being a Short but Complete Description of the Duties of the Young Engineer in the Preliminary and Location Surveys and in Construction. Fourth edition, revised and enlarged. Illustrated, 12mo, cloth....... 2 00

CLARK (D. KINNEAR, C.E.) A Manual of Rules, Tables and Data for Mechanical Engineers. Illustrated with numerous diagrams. 1012 pages. 8vo, cloth 5 00
Half morocco.... ... . 7 50

—— Fuel; its Combustion and Economy, consisting of abridgments of Treatise on the Combustion of Coal. By C. W. Williams; and the Economy of Fuel, by T. S. Prideaux With extensive additions in recent practice in the Combustion and Economy of Fuel, Coal, Coke, Wood, Peat, Petroleum, etc. 12mo, cloth. 1 50

DORR (B. F.) The Surveyor's Guide and Pocket Table Book. 18mo, morocco flaps. Second edition 2 00

DUBOIS (A. J.) The New Method of Graphic Statics. With 60 illustrations. 8vo, cloth 1 50

EDDY (Prof. H. T.) Researches in Graphical Statics. Embracing New Constructions in Graphical Statics, a New General Method in Graphical Statics, and the Theory of Internal Stress in Graphical Statics. 8vo, cloth 1 50

—— Maximum Stresses under Concentrated Loads. Treated graphically. Illustrated. 8vo, cloth 1 50

EISSLER (M.) The Metallurgy of Gold; a Practical Treatise on the Metallurgical Treatment of Gold-Bearing Ores. 187 illustrations. 12mo, cl 5 00

—— The Metallurgy of Silver; a Practical Treatise on the Amalgamation, Roasting, and Lixiviation of Silver Ores. 124 illustrations. 12mo, cloth 4 00

—— The Metallurgy of Argentiferous Lead; a Practical Treatise on the Smelting of Silver Lead Ores and the refining of Lead Bullion. With 183 illustrations. 8vo, cloth 5 00

ELIOT (Prof. C. W.) and STORER (Prof. F. H.) A Compendious Manual of Qualitative Chemical Analysis. Revised with the co-operation of the authors, by Prof. William R. Nichols. Illustrated. 17th edition. Newly revised by Prof. W. B. Lindsay. 12mo, cloth 1 50

EVERETT (J. D.) Elementary Text-book of Physics. Illustrated. 12mo, cloth 1 40

FANNING (J. T.) A Practical Treatise on Hydraulic and Water-supply Engineering. Relating to the Hydrology, Hydrodynamics, and Practical Construction of Water-works in North America. Illustrated. 8vo, cloth 5 00

FISKE (Lieut. BRADLEY A., U. S. N.) Electricity in Theory and Practice; or, The Elements of Electrical Engineering. 8vo, cloth 2 50

FLEMING (Prof. A. J.) The Alternate Current Transformer in Theory and Practice. Vol. I.—The Induction of Electric Currents. Illustrated. 8vo, cloth.... 3 00

SCIENTIFIC PUBLICATIONS. 7

FOLEY (NELSON), and THOS. PRAY, Jr. The Mechanical Engineers' Reference-book for Machine and Boiler Construction, in two parts. Part I—General Engineering Data. Part 2—Boiler Construction. With fifty-one plates and numerous illustrations, specially drawn for this work. Folio, half mor. ...25 00

FORNEY (MATTHIAS N.) Catechism of the Locomotive. Revised and enlarged. 8vo, cloth. 3 50

FOSTER (Gen. J. G., U. S. A.) Submarine Blasting in Boston Harbor, Massachusetts. Removal of Tower and Corwin Rocks. Illustrated with 7 plates. 4to, cloth.... .. .. 3 5.

FRANCIS (Jas. B., C.E.) Lowell Hydraulic Experiments. Being a selection from experiments on Hydraulic Motors, on the Flow of Water over Weirs, in open Canals of uniform rectangular section, and through submerged Orifices and diverging Tubes. Made at Lowell, Mass Illustrated 4to. cloth .15 00

GERBER (NICHOLAS). Chemical and Physical Analysis of Milk, Condensed Milk, and Infant's Milk-Food. 8vo, cloth. 1 25

GILLMORE (Gen. Q. A.) Treatise on Limes, Hydraulic Cements, and Mortars. With numerous illustrations. 8vo, cloth.... .... 4 00

—— Practical Treatise on the Construction of Roads, Streets, and Pavements. With 70 illustrations. 12mo, cloth... .. .. 2 00

—— Report on Strength of the Building-Stones in the United States, etc. Illustrated. 8vo, cloth. 1 00

GOODEVE (T. M.) A Text-book on the Steam-Engine With a Supplement on Gas-Engines. 143 illustrations. 12mo, cloth. 2 00

GORE (G., F.R.S.) The Art of Electrolytic Separation of Metals, etc. (Theoretical and Practical.) Illustrated. 8vo, cloth 3 50

GORDON (J. E. H.) School Electricity Illustrations. 12mo, cloth.... .... 2 00

SCIENTIFIC PUBLICATIONS.   9

HERRMANN (GUSTAV). The Graphical Statics of Mechanism. A Guide for the Use of Machinists, Architects, and Engineers ; and also a Text-book for Technical Schools. Translated and annotated by A. P. Smith, M.E. 12mo, cloth, 7 folding plates..... 2 00

HEWSON (WM.) Principles and Practice of Embanking Lands from River Floods, as applied to the Levees of the Mississippi. 8vo, cloth............................ 2 00

HENRICI (OLAUS). Skeleton Structures, Applied to the Building of Steel and Iron Bridges. Illustrated.. 1 50

HOBBS (W. R. P.) The Arithmetic of Electrical Measurements, with numerous examples. 12mo, cloth.... 50

HOLLEY (ALEXANDER L.) Railway Practice. American and European Railway practice in the Economical Generation of Steam, including the Materials and Construction of Coal-burning Boilers, Combustion, the Variable Blast, Vaporization, Circulation, Superheating, Supplying and Heating Feed-water, etc., and the Adaptation of Wood and Coke-burning Engines to Coal-burning; and in Permanent Way, including Road-bed, Sleepers, Rails, Joint Fastenings, Street Railways, etc. With 77 lithographed plates. Folio, cloth.................................12 00

HOLMES (A. BROMLEY). The Electric Light Popularly Explained. Fifth edition. Illustrated. 12mo, paper. 40

HOWARD (C. R.) Earthwork Mensuration on the Basis of the Prismoidal Formulæ. Containing Simple and Labor-saving Method of obtaining Prismoidal Contents directly from End Areas. Illustrated by Examples and accompanied by Plain Rules for Practical Uses. Illustrated. 8vo, cloth.. .... 1 50

HUMBER (WILLIAM, C. E.) A Handy Book for the Calculation of Strains in Girders, and Similar Structures, and their Strength ; Consisting of Formulæ and Corresponding Diagrams, with numerous details for practical application, etc. Fourth edition. 12mo, cloth.. 2 50

HUTTON (W. S.) Steam-Boiler Construction. A Practical Hand-book for Engineers, Boiler Makers, and Steam Users. With upwards of 300 illustrations. 8vo, cloth 7 00

ISHERWOOD (B. F.) Engineering Precedents for Steam Machinery. Arranged in the most practical and useful manner for Engineers. With illustrations. 2 vols. in 1. 8vo, cloth....... .... 2 50

JAMIESON (ANDREW, C.E.) A Text-book on Steam and Steam-Engines. Illustrated. 12mo, cloth....... 3 00

JANNETTAZ (EDWARD). A Guide to the Determination of Rocks; being an Introduction to Lithology. Translated from the French by Professor G. W. Plympton. 12mo, cloth............................. 1 50

JONES (H. CHAPMAN). Text-book of Experimental Organic Chemistry for Students. 18mo, cloth........ 1 00

JOYNSON (F. H.) The Metals used in Construction. Iron, Steel, Bessemer Metal, etc. Illustrated. 12mo, cloth................... 75

—— Designing and Construction of Machine Gearing. Illustrated. 8vo, cloth................................. 2 00

KANSAS CITY BRIDGE (THE). With an Account of the Regimen of the Missouri River and a Description of the Methods used for Founding in that River. By O. Chanute, Chief Engineer, and George Morrison, Assistant Engineer. Illustrated with 5 lithographic views and 12 plates of plans. 4to, cloth.............. 6 00

KAPP (GISBERT, C.E.) Electric Transmission of Energy and its Transformation, Subdivision, and Distribution. A Practical Hand-book. 12mo, cloth..... 3 00

KEMPE (H. R.) The Electrical Engineer's Pocket Book of Modern Rules, Formulæ, Tables, and Data. Illustrated. 32mo, mor. gilt........................ 1 75

ENNELLEY (A. E.) Theoretical Elements of Electro-Dynamic Machinery. Vol. I. Illustrated. 8vo, cloth. 1 50

ING (W. H.) Lessons and Practical Notes on Steam. The Steam-Engine, Propellers, etc., for Young Marine Engineers, Students, and others. Revised by Chief Engineer J. W. King, United States Navy. 8vo, cloth ....:....... .... 2 00

KIRKALDY (WM. G.) Illustrations of David Kirkaldy's System of Mechanical Testing, as Originated and Carried On by him during a Quarter of a Century.

Comprising a Large Selection of Tabulated Results, showing the Strength and other Properties of Materials used in Construction, with Explanatory Text and Historical Sketch. Numerous engravings and 25 lithographed plates. 4to, cloth........................25 00

KIRKWOOD (JAS. P.) Report on the Filtration of River Waters for the supply of Cities, as practised in Europe. Illustrated by 30 double-plate engravings. 4to, cloth...15 00

LARRABEE (C. S.) Cipher and Secret Letter and Telegraphic Code, with Hog's Improvements. 18mo, cloth... 60

LARDEN (W., M. A.) A School Course on Heat. 12mo, half leather.. 2 00

LEITZE (ERNST). Modern Heliographic Processes. A Manual of Instruction in the Art of Reproducing Drawings, Engravings, etc., by the action of Light. With 32 wood-cuts and ten specimens of Heliograms. 8vo, cloth. Second edition............................ 3 00

LOCKWOOD (THOS. D.) Electricity, Magnetism, and Electro-Telegraphy. A Practical Guide for Students, Operators, and Inspectors. 8vo, cloth. Third edition... 2 50

LODGE (OLIVER J.) Elementary Mechanics, including Hydrostatics and Pneumatics. Revised edition. 12mo, cloth... 1 20

LOCKE (ALFRED G. and CHARLES G.) A Practical Treatise on the Manufacture of Sulphuric Acid. With 77 Constructive Plates drawn to Scale Measurements, and other Illustrations. Royal 8vo, cloth.....15 00

LOVELL (D. H.) Practical Switch Work. A Handbook for Track Foremen. Illustrated. 12mo, cloth.. 1 50

LUNGE (GEO.) A Theoretical and Practical Treatise on the Manufacture of Sulphuric Acid and Alkali with the Collateral Branches. Vol. I. Sulphuric Acid. Second edition, revised and enlarged. 342 Illustrations. 8vo., cloth...15 00

——— and HUNTER F.) The Alkali Maker's Pocket-Book. Tables and Analytical Methods for Manufacturers of Sulphuric Acid, Nitric Acid, Soda, Potash ... Second edition. 12mo, cloth......... 3 00

MACCORD (Prof. C. W.) A Practical T... ...on the Slide-Valve by Eccentrics, examining by methods the action of the Eccentric upon the Slide-Valve, and explaining the practical processes of laying out the movements, adapting the Valve for its various duties in the Steam-Engine. Illustrated. 4to, cloth... ..... 2 50

MAYER (Prof. A. M.) Lecture Notes on Physics. 8vo. cloth.. .... 2 00

McCULLOCH (Prof. R. S.) Elementary Treatise on the Mechanical Theory of Heat, and its application to Air and Steam Engines. 8vo, cloth 3 50

MERRILL (Col. WM. E., U. S. A.) Iron Truss Bridges for Railroads. The method of calculating strains in Trusses, with a careful comparison of the most prominent Trusses, in reference to economy in combination, etc. Illustrated. 4to, cloth............ ... . 5 00

METAL TURNING. By a Foreman Pattern Maker. Illustrated with 81 engravings. 12mo, cloth......... 1 50

MINIFIE (WM.) Mechanical Drawing. A Text-book of Geometrical Drawing for the use of Mechanics and schools, in which the Definitions and Rules of Geometry are familiarly explained ; the Practical Problems are arranged from the most simple to the more complex, and in their description technicalities are avoided as much as possible. With illustrations for Drawing Plans, Sections, and Elevations of Railways and Machinery ; an Introduction to Isometrical Drawing, and an Essay on Linear Perspective and Shadows. Illustrated with over 200 diagrams engraved on steel. With an appendix on the Theory and Application of Colors. 8vo, cloth. ....:........... 4 00

——— Geometrical Drawing. Abridged from the octavo edition, for the use of schools. Illustrated with 48 steel plates. Ninth edition. 12mo, cloth 2 00

MODERN METEOROLOGY. A Series of Six Lectures, delivered under the auspices of the Meteorological Society in 1878. Illustrated. 12mo, cloth............ 1 50

MOONEY (WM.) The American Gas Engineers' and Superintendents' Hand-book, consisting of Rules, Reference Tables, and original matter pertaining to the Manufacture, Manipulation, and Distribution of Illuminating Gas. Illustrated. 12mo, morocco . .. 3 00

MOTT (H. A., Jun.) A Practical Treatise on Chemistry (Qualitative and Quantitative Analysis), Stoichiometry, Blow-pipe Analysis, Mineralogy, Assaying, Pharmaceutical Preparations, Human Secretions, Specific Gravities, Weights and Measures, etc. New Edition, 1883. 650 pages. 8vo, cloth............ .... 4 00

MULLIN (JOSEPH P., M.E.) Modern Moulding and Pattern-making. A Practical Treatise upon Pattern-Shop and Foundry Work: embracing the Moulding of Pulleys, Spur Gears, Worm Gears, Balance-wheels, Stationary Engine and Locomotive Cylinders, Globe Valves, Tool Work, Mining Machinery, Screw Propellers, Pattern-shop Machinery, and the latest improvements in English and American Cupolas; together with a large collection of original and carefully selected Rules and Tables for every-day use in the Drawing Office, Pattern-shop, and Foundry. 12mo, cloth, illustrated........ .... 2 50

MUNRO (JOHN, C.E.) and JAMIESON (ANDREW, C.E.) A Pocket-book of Electrical Rules and Tables for the use of Electricians and Engineers. Seventh edition, revised and enlarged. With numerous diagrams. Pocket size. Leather 2 50

MURPHY (J. G., M.E.) Practical Mining. A Field Manual for Mining Engineers. With Hints for Investors in Mining Properties. 16mo, morocco tucks.. 1 50

NAQUET (A.) Legal Chemistry. A Guide to the Detection of Poisons, Falsification of Writings, Adulteration of Alimentary and Pharmaceutical Substances, Analysis of Ashes, and examination of Hair. Coins, Arms, and Stains, as applied to Chemical Jurisprudence, for the use of Chemists, Physicians, Lawyers, Pharmacists and Experts. Translated, with additions, including a list of books and memoirs on Toxicology, etc., from the French, by J. P. Battershall, Ph.D., with a preface by C. F. Chandler, Ph.D., M.D., LL.D. 12mo, cloth. 2 00

NEWALL (J. W.) Plain Practical Directions for Drawing, Sizing and Cutting Bevel-Gears, showing how the Teeth may be cut in a plain Milling Machine or Gear Cutter so as to give them a correct shape, from end to end; and showing how to get out all particulars for the Workshop without making any Drawings. Including a full set of Tables of Reference. Folding Plates, 8vo., cloth. 3 00

NEWLANDS (JAMES). The Carpenter's and Joiners' Assistant: being a Comprehensive Treatise on the Selection, Preparation and Strength of Materials, and the Mechanical Principles of Framing, with their application in Carpentry, Joinery, and Hand-Railing; also, a Complete Treatise on Sines; and an illustrated Glossary of Terms used in Architecture and Building. Illustrated. Folio, half mor........................15 00

NIBLETT (J. T.) Secondary Batteries. Illustrated. 12mo, cloth 1 50

NIPHER (FRANCIS E., A.M.) Theory of Magnetic Measurements, with an appendix on the Method of Least Squares. 12mo, cloth....................... 1 00

NOAD (HENRY M.) The Students' Text-book of Electricity. A new edition, carefully revised. With an Introduction and additional chapters by W. H. Preece. With 471 illustrations. 12mo, cloth......... 4 00

NUGENT (E.) Treatise on Optics; or, Light and Sight theoretically and practically treated, with the application to Fine Art and Industrial Pursuits. With 103 illustrations. 12mo. cloth............................. 1 50

PAGE (DAVID). The Earth's Crust, a Handy Outline of Geology. 16mo, cloth............................. 75

PARSONS (Jr., W. B., C.E.) Track, a Complete Manual of Maintenance of Way, according to the Latest and Best Practice on Leading American Railroads. Illustrated. 8vo, cloth 2 00

PEIRCE (B.) System of Analytic Mechanics. 4to, cloth 10 00

PHILLIPS (JOSHUA). Engineering Chemistry. A Practical Treatise for the use of Analytical Chemists, Engineers, Iron Masters, Iron Founders, students and others. Comprising methods of Analysis and Valuation of the principal materials used in Engineering works, with numerous Analyses, Examples and Suggestions. 314 Illustrations. 8vo, cloth.............. 4 00

PLANE TABLE (THE). Its Uses in Topographical Surveying. Illustrated. 8vo, cloth.................. 2 00

PLATTNER. Manual of Qualitative and Quantitative Analysis with the Blow-pipe. From the last German edition, revised and enlarged, by Prof. Th. Richter, of the Royal Saxon Mining Academy. Translated by

Prof. H. B. Cornwall, assisted by John H. Caswell. Illustrated with 87 wood-cuts and one lithographic plate. Fourth edition, revised. 560 pages. 8vo, cloth...... 5 00

PLANTE (GASTON). The Storage of Electrical Energy, and Researches in the Effects created by Currents, combining Quantity with High Tension. Translated from the French by Paul B. Elwell. 89 illustrations. 8vo............ 4 00

PLYMPTON (Prof. GEO. W.) The Blow-pipe. A Guide to its use in the Determination of Salts and Minerals. Compiled from various sources. 12mo, cloth............ 1 50

POCKET LOGARITHMS to Four Places of Decimals, including Logarithms of Numbers and Logarithmic Sines and Tangents to Single Minutes. To which is added a Table of Natural Sines, Tangents and Co-Tangents. 16mo, boards............ 50

POPE (F. L.) Modern Practice of the Electric Telegraph. A Technical Hand-book for Electricians, Managers and Operators. New edition, rewritten and enlarged, and fully illustrated. 8vo, cloth....... 1 50

PRAY (Jr., THOMAS). Twenty Years with the Indicator; being a Practical Text-book for the Engineer or the Student. Illustrated. 8vo, cloth............ 2 50

PRACTICAL IRON-FOUNDING. By the author of "Pattern Making," etc., etc. Illustrated with over one hundred engravings. 12mo, cloth............ 1 50

PREECE (W H.) and STUBBS (A. J.) Manual of Telephony. Illustrations and Plates. 12mo, cloth........ 4 50

PRESCOTT (Prof. A. B.) Organic Analysis. A Manual of the Descriptive and Analytical Chemistry of certain Carbon Compounds in Common Use; a Guide in the Qualitative and Quantitative Analysis of Organic Materials in Commercial and Pharmaceutical Assays, in the estimation of Impurities under Authorized Standards, and in Forensic Examinations for Poisons, with Directions for Elementary Organic Analysis. 8vo, cloth........ 5 00

—— Outlines of Proximate Organic Analysis, for the Identification. Separation, and Quantitative Determination of the more commonly occurring Organic Compounds. 12mo, cloth 1 75

PRESCOTT (Prof. A. B.) First Book in Qualitative Chemistry. Fifth edition. 12mo, cloth 1 50
—— and OTIS COE JOHNSON. Qualitative Chemical Analysis. A Guide in the Practical Study of Chemistry and in the work of Analysis. Revised edition With Descriptive Chemistry extended throughout.... 3 50
PRITCHARD (O. G.) The Manufacture of Electric Light Carbons. Illustrated. 8vo, paper........ 60
PULSIFER (W. H.) Notes for a History of Lead. 8vo, cloth, gilt tops 4 00
PYNCHON (Prof. T. R.) Introduction to Chemical Physics, designed for the use of Academies, Colleges, and High Schools. 269 illustrations on wood. Crown 8vo, cloth 3 00
RANDALL (J. E.) A Practical Treatise on the Incandescent Lamp. Illustrated. 16mo, cloth............ 50
—— (P. M.) Quartz Operator's Hand-book. New edition, revised and enlarged, fully illustrated. 12mo, cloth... 2 00
RAFTER (GEO. W.) Sewage Disposal in the United States. Illustrated. 8vo, cloth.................... 6 00
RANKINE (W. J. MACQUORN, C.E., LL.D., F.R.S.) Applied Mechanics. Comprising the Principles of Statics and Cinematics, and Theory of Structures, Mechanism, and Machines. With numerous diagrams. Thoroughly revised by W. J. Millar. Crown 8vo, cloth....................................... 5 00
—— Civil Engineering. Comprising Engineering Surveys, Earthwork, Foundations, Masonry, Carpentry, Metal-work, Roads, Railways, Canals, Rivers, Water-Works, Harbors, etc. With numerous tables and illustrations. Thoroughly revised by W. J. Millar. Crown 8vo, cloth........ .. .. 6 50
—— Machinery and Millwork. Comprising the Geometry, Motions, Work, Strength, Construction, and Objects of Machines, etc. Illustrated with nearly 300 woodcuts. Thoroughly revised by W. J. Miller. Crown 8vo, cloth....... .... 5 00
—— The Steam-Engine and Other Prime Movers. With diagram of the Mechanical Properties of Steam, folding plates, numerous tables and illustrations. Thoroughly revised by W. J. Millar. Crown 8vo, cloth... 5 00

RANKINE (W. J. MACQUORN, C.E., LL.D., F.R.S.) Useful Rules and Tables for Engineers and Others. With Appendix, tables, tests, and formulæ for the use of Electrical Engineers. Comprising Submarine Electrical Engineering, Electric Lighting, and Transmission of Power. By Andrew Jamieson, C.E., F.R.S.E. Thoroughly revised by W. J. Millar. Crown 8vo, cloth 4 00

—— A Mechanical Text-book. By Prof. Macquorn Rankine and E. F. Bamber, C.E. With numerous illustrations. Crown, 8vo, cloth. 3 50

REED'S ENGINEERS' HAND-BOOK, to the Local Marine Board Examinations for Certificates of Competency as First and Second Class Engineers. By W. H. Thorn. Illustrated. 8vo, cloth. 4 50

RICE (Prof. J. M.) and JOHNSON (Prof. W. W.) On a New Method of obtaining the Differential of Functions, with especial reference to the Newtonian Conception of Rates or Velocities. 12mo, paper......... 50

RIPPER (WILLIAM). A Course of Instruction in Machine Drawing and Design for Technical Schools and Engineer Students. With 52 plates and numerous explanatory engravings. Folio, cloth............... 7 50

ROEBLING (J. A.) Long and Short Span Railway Bridges. Illustrated with large copperplate engravings of plans and views. Imperial folio, cloth........25 00

ROGERS (Prof. H. D.) The Geology of Pennsylvania. A Government Survey, with a General View of the Geology of the United States, essays on the Coal Formation and its Fossils, and a description of the Coal Fields of North America and Great Britain. Illustrated with plates and engravings in the text. 3 vols. 4to, cloth, with portfolio of maps...............15 00

ROSE (JOSHUA, M.E) The Pattern-makers' Assistant. Embracing Lathe Work, Branch Work, Core Work, Sweep Work, and Practical Gear Constructions, the Preparation and Use of Tools, together with a large collection of useful and valuable Tables. Sixth edition. Illustrated with 250 engravings. 8vo. cloth. 2 50

—— Key to Engines and Engine-Running. A Practical Treatise upon the Management of Steam Engines and Boilers, for the Use of Those who Desire to Pass an Examination to Take Charge of an Engine or Boiler. With numerous illustrations, and Instructions upon Engineers' Calculations, Indicators, Diagrams, Engine Adjustments, and other Valuable Information necessary for Engineers and Firemen. 12mo, cloth.. 3 00

SABINE (ROBERT). History and Progress of the Electric Telegraph. With descriptions of some of the apparatus. 12mo, cloth............................ 1 25

SAELTZER (ALEX.) Treatise on Acoustics in connection with Ventilation. 12mo, cloth................. 1 00

SALOMONS (Sir DAVID, M. A.) Electric Light Installations. Vol. I. The management of Accumulators. Seventh edition, revised and enlarged, with numerous illustrations. 12mo, cloth.......................... 1 50

SAUNNIER, (CLAUDIUS). Watchmaker's Hand-book. A Workshop Companion for those engaged in Watchmaking and allied Mechanical Arts. Translated by J. Tripplin and E. Rigg. 12mo, cloth................ 3 50

SEATON (A. E.) A Manual of Marine Engineering. Comprising the Designing, Construction and Working of Marine Machinery. With numerous tables and illustrations. 10th edition. 8vo, cloth............... 5 00

SCHUMANN (F.) A Manual of Heating and Ventilation in its Practical Application, for the use of Engineers and Architects. Embracing a series of Tables and Formulæ for dimensions of heating, flow and return pipes for steam and hot-water boilers, flues, etc. 12mo, illustrated, full roan..................... 1 50

—— Formulas and Tables for Architects and Engineers in calculating the strains and capacity of structures in Iron and Wood. 12mo, morocco, tucks............... 1 50

SCRIBNER (J. M.) Engineers' and Mechanics' Companion. Comprising United States Weights and Measures, Mensuration of Superfices, and Solids, Tables of Squares and Cubes, Square and Cube Roots, Circumference and Areas of Circles, the Mechanical Powers, Centres of Gravity, Gravitation of Bodies. Pendulums, Specific Gravity of Bodies, Strength, Weight, and Crush of Materials, Water-Wheels, Hydrostatics, Hydraulics, Statics, Centres of

Percussion and Gyration, Friction Heat, Tables of the Weight of Metals, Scantling, etc. Steam and the Steam-Engine. 16mo, full morocco.......... .. .. 1 50

SCHELLEN (Dr. H.) Magneto-Electric and Dynamo-Electric Machines: their Construction and Practical Application to Electric Lighting, and the Transmission of Power. Translated from the third German edition by N. S. Keith and Percy Neymann, Ph.D. With very large additions and notes relating to American Machines, by N. S. Keith. Vol. 1, with 353 illustrations....... .... 5 00

SHIELDS (J. E.) Notes on Engineering Construction. Embracing Discussions of the Principles involved, and Descriptions of the Material employed in Tunnelling, Bridging, Canal and Road Building, etc. 12mo, cloth........... .... 1 50

SHREVE (S. H.) A Treatise on the Strength of Bridges and Roofs. Comprising the determination of Algebraic formulas for strains in Horizontal, Inclined or Rafter, Triangular, Bowstring, Lenticular, and other Trusses, from fixed and moving loads, with practical applications, and examples, for the use of Students and Engineers. 87 woodcut illustrations. 8vo, cloth. 3 50

SHUNK (W. F.) The Field Engineer. A Handy Book of Practice in the Survey, Location, and Truck-work of Railroads, containing a large collection of Rules and Tables. original and selected, applicable to both the Standard and Narrow Gauge, and prepared with special reference to the wants of the young Engineer. Ninth edition. Revised and Enlarged. 12mo, morocco, tucks. 2 50

SIMMS (F. W.) A Treatise on the Principles and Practice of Levelling. Showing its application to purposes of Railway Engineering, and the Construction of Roads, etc. Revised and corrected. with the addition of Mr. Laws' Practical Examples for setting out Railway Curves. Illustrated. 8vo, cloth......... ... 2 50

——— Practical Tunnelling. Explaining in detail Setting-out of the Work, Shaft-sinking, Sub-excavating, Timbering, etc., with cost of work. 8vo, cloth........... 7 50

THE VAN NOSTRAND SCIENCE SERIES.

No. 81.--WATER METERS: COMPARATIVE TESTS OF ACCURACY, DELIVERY, ETC. Distinctive features of the Worthington, Kennedy, Siemens, and Hesse meters. By Ross E. Browne.

No. 82.--THE PRESERVATION OF TIMBER BY THE USE OF ANTISEPTICS. By Samuel Bagster Boulton, C. E.

No. 83.--MECHANICAL INTEGRATORS. By Prof. Henry S. H. SHAW, C. E.

No. 84.--FLOW OF WATER IN OPEN CHANNELS, PIPES, CONDUITS, SEWERS, ETC. With Tables. By P. J. Flynn, C. E.

No. 85.--THE LUMINIFEROUS ÆTHER. By Prof. de Volson Wood.

No. 86.--HAND-BOOK OF MINERALOGY: DETERMINATION AND DESCRIPTION OF MINERALS FOUND IN THE UNITED STATES. By Prof. J. C. Foye. Fourth edition, revised.

No. 87.--TREATISE ON THE THEORY OF THE CONSTRUCTION OF HELICOIDAL OBLIQUE ARCHES. By John L. Culley, C. E.

No. 88.--BEAMS AND GIRDERS. Practical Formulas for their Resistance. By P. H. Philbrick.

No. 89.--MODERN GUN COTTON: ITS MANUFACTURE, PROPERTIES, AND ANALYSIS. By Lieut. John P. Wisser, U. S. A.

No. 90.--ROTARY MOTION AS APPLIED TO THE GYROSCOPE. By Gen. J. G. Barnard.

No. 91.-- LEVELING: BAROMETRIC TRIGONOMETRIC AND SPIRIT. By Prof. I. O. Baker.

No. 92.--PETROLEUM: ITS PRODUCTION AND USE. By Boverton Redwood, F. I. C., F. C. S.

No. 93.--RECENT PRACTICE IN THE SANITARY DRAINAGE OF BUILDINGS. With Memoranda on the Cost of Plumbing Work. Second edition, revised. By William Paul Gerhard, C. E.

No. 94.--THE TREATMENT OF SEWAGE. By Dr. C. Meymott Tidy.

No. 95.--PLATE GIRDER CONSTRUCTION. By Isami Hiroi, C. E. 2d edition, revised and enlarged.

No. 96.--ALTERNATE CURRENT MACHINERY. By Gisbert Kapp, Assoc. M. Inst., C. E.

No. 97.-- THE DISPOSAL OF HOUSEHOLD WASTES. By W. Paul Gerhard, Sanitary Engineer.

No. 98.--PRACTICAL DYNAMO BUILDING FOR AMATEURS. HOW TO WIND FOR ANY OUTPUT. By Frederick Walker. Fully illustrated.

No. 99--TRIPLE-EXPANSION ENGINES AND ENGINE TRIALS. By Prof. Osborne Reynolds. Edited, with notes, etc., by F. E. Idell, M. E.

THE VAN NOSTRAND SCIENCE SERIES.

No. 100.—HOW TO BECOME AN ENGINEER, or the Theoretical and Practical Training necessary in fitting for the duties of the Civil Engineer. By Prof. Geo. W. Plympton.

No. 101.—THE SEXTANT, and other Reflecting Mathematical Instruments. With Practical Hints for their adjustment and use. By F. R. Brainard, U. S. Navy.

No. 102.—THE GALVANIC CIRCUIT INVESTIGATED MATHEMATICALLY. By Dr. G. S. Ohm, Berlin, 1827. Translated by William Francis. With Preface and Notes by the Editor, Thomas D. Lockwood, M.I.E.E.

No. 103.—THE MICROSCOPICAL EXAMINATION OF POTABLE WATER. With Diagrams. By Geo. W. Rafter.

No. 104.—VAN NOSTRAND'S TABLE BOOK FOR CIVIL AND MECHANICAL ENGINEERS. Compiled by Prof. Geo. W. Plympton

No. 105.—DETERMINANTS. An Introduction to the Study of, with Examples and Applications. By Prof. G. A. Miller.

No. 106.—COMPRESSED AIR. Experiments upon the Transmission of Power by Compressed Air in Paris. (Popp's System.) By Prof. A. B. W. Kennedy. The Transmission and Distribution of Power from Central Stations by Compressed Air. By Prof. W. C. Unwin.

No. 107.—A GRAPHICAL METHOD FOR SWING-BRIDGES. A Rational and Easy Graphical Analysis of the Stresses in Ordinary Swing-Bridges. With an Introduction on the General Theory of Graphical Statics. By Benjamin F. La Rue. 4 Plates.

No. 108.—SLIDE VALVE DIAGRAMS. A French Method for Constructing Slide Valve Diagrams. By Lloyd Bankson, B S., Assistant Naval Constructor, U. S. Navy. 8 Folding Plates.

No. 109.—THE MEASUREMENT OF ELECTRIC CURRENTS. Electrical Measuring Instruments. By James Swinburne. Meters for Electrical Energy. By C. H. Wordingham. Edited, with Preface, by T. Commerford Martin. Folding Plate and numerous illustrations.

No. 110.—TRANSITION CURVES. A Field-Book for Engineers, containing Rules and Tables for Laying out Transition Curves. By Walter G. Fox, C.E.

No. 111.—GAS-LIGHTING AND GAS-FITTING. Specifications and Rules for Gas-Piping. Notes on the advantages of Gas for Cooking and Heating, and Useful Hints to Gas Consumers. Second edition, rewritten and enlarged. By Wm. Paul Gerhard, C. E.

No. 112.—A PRIMER ON THE CALCULUS. By E. Sherman Gould, M. Am. Soc. C. E.

THE VAN NOSTRAND SCIENCE SERIES.

No. 113.—PHYSICAL PROBLEMS and their Solution. By A. Bourgougnon, formerly Assistant at Bellevue Hospital.

No. 114.—MANUAL OF THE SLIDE RULE. By F. A. Halsey, of the *American Machinist*.

No. 115.—TRAVERSE TABLE, showing the difference of Latitude and Departure for distances between 1 and 100 and for Angles to Quarter Degrees between 1 degree and 90 degrees. (Reprinted from Scribner's Pocket Table Book.)

www.ingramcontent.com/pod-product-compliance
Lightning Source LLC
Chambersburg PA
CBHW020105170426
43199CB00009B/404